dlife
JOURNAL
NEW TESTAMENT 1

Property of:

_____

Published by Life Bible Study

Life Bible Study LLC is a Christian publisher serving churches and Christian communities in order to advance the Gospel of Jesus Christ, making disciples as we go.

© 2017 Life Bible Study
D-Life Journal: New Testament 1 by Dr. Bill Wilks
Publisher Dr. John Herring

ISBN-13: 978-1-63204-069-5
ISBN-10: 1-63204-069-7
LifeBibleStudy.com

Printed in the United States of America
1 2 3 4 5 6 / 22 21 20 19 18 17

TABLE OF CONTENTS

Introduction .... *v*
S-P-A-C-E Bible Study Method .... *vii*
The Ministry of D-Life .... *ix*

Week 1 1
Week 2 5
Week 3 9
Week 4 13
Week 5 17
Week 6 21
Week 7 25
Week 8 29
Week 9 33
Week 10 37
Week 11 41
Week 12 45
Week 13 49
Week 14 53
Week 15 57
Week 16 61
Week 17 65
Week 18 69
Week 19 73
Week 20 77
Week 21 81
Week 22 85
Week 23 89
Week 24 93
Week 25 97
Week 26 101

Week 27 105
Week 28 109
Week 29 113
Week 30 117
Week 31 121
Week 32 125
Week 33 129
Week 34 133
Week 35 137
Week 36 141
Week 37 145
Week 38 149
Week 39 153
Week 40 157
Week 41 161
Week 42 165
Week 43 169
Week 44 173
Week 45 177
Week 46 181
Week 47 185
Week 48 189
Week 49 193
Week 50 197
Week 51 201
Week 52 205

Author Bio 209

INTRODUCTION

Jesus charged His disciples with making disciples (Matthew 28:19), baptizing in His name and teaching them His commandments. That charge is just as relevant today as it was to the first-century church. Becoming a disciple is more than being saved and baptized. Becoming a disciple involves learning to follow God by carefully and diligently studying God's Word and then by intentionally living God's Word for others to see.

Discipleship is a journey and life-long process. It involves daily seeking to know God's heart, studying God's Word, and then living out God's expectations. It is not an easy journey, but it is more rewarding than any other endeavor in this life.

D-Life Journal is a discipleship tool that can be used as a guide for personal spiritual growth or in a discipleship group. Groups can begin with as few as three to five members. New groups should be started when a group enrollment reaches eight. To begin a discipleship group, consider creating diversity within the group, such as:

- New believers, who can benefit by connecting in discipleship to other believers.

- Unbelievers, nonbelievers, and the unchurched, who are open to hearing about Jesus.

- Multi-generational believers, who bring different life stages and different spiritual journeys into the group.

- Believers struggling in life with issues such as drug abuse, depression, and gender identification, who will benefit from having the support and accountability of other believers.

HOW TO LEAD A D-LIFE GROUP:

- ***Fellowship Time*** – Create fellowship within the group wherever it meets—a coffee shop, café, home, park, school, or church. Share coffee, a snack, or a meal.

- ***Accountability Time*** – Create accountability each week by asking if group members read their Bibles daily. Lead them to share some application points written in their notes.

- ***Prayer Time*** – Develop an on-going emphasis on prayer, with members taking responsibility for leading the group in prayer, praying for specific prayer requests, and praying for revival in our land.

- ***Tell the Story*** – Assign a member in the group each week to tell the biblical story or paraphrase the passage to be studied in his or her own words.

- ***Read the Story*** – Assign another member in the group to read the passage to be studied from the Bible. See if anything was left out of the storytelling.

- ***Facilitate Bible Study*** – Assign another member in your group to facilitate the Bible study using the questions provided in the weekly study guide.

  When facilitating, use the study guide questions with intention. When time is an issue, use only 3 to 5 questions and work to intentionally involve all group members in discussion. Keep the discussion on point. Be truthful, positive, and transparent. Clearly address theological issues when necessary. Be sensitive to the Holy Spirit.

- ***Ministry Planning Time*** – Spend a few minutes planning for your next ministry project. You will do one ministry and evangelism project every two months.

- ***Weekly Assignments*** –Assign tasks for the next week to different members of the group: lead in prayer, tell the story, read the story, and facilitate the Bible study.

S-P-A-C-E BIBLE STUDY METHOD

A major goal of D-Life is to lead people to develop a life long habit of daily Bible reading. This alone is life changing. Each day we want to make SPACE in our hearts for God's Word by writing down one personal application point from our daily Bible reading assignments. We make **S-P-A-C-E** by asking five simple questions as we read each chapter. Ask, is there a:

- **S**in to confess?
- **P**romise to claim?
- **A**ttitude to change?
- **C**ommand to obey?
- **E**xample to follow?

In each chapter you will find an answer to at least one of these question. Ask God to give you a personal word as you read. Let the Holy Spirit speak to your heart. As you ask these questions, let God show you a personal point of application. Psalm 119:18 is a great prayer to pray, "Open my eyes, that I may behold wondrous things out of your law."

When God speaks to your heart, you want to write it down. In your journal, circle the appropriate letter in the acrostic **S-P-A-C-E** that relates to your application point and write a brief note reflecting your thoughts. For example, in John 3:16, you may see a "Promise to claim." Circle the letter "P" and then you may write something like: "What a great promise to claim! God loves me and has given me eternal life through faith in His Son. Thank you God for your incredible gift to me."

It's helpful to have a certain time and place where you meet alone with God each day for prayer and Bible reading. Make your daily time alone with God a major priority in your life.

Taken from Rick Warren's Bible Study Methods: Twelve Ways You Can Unlock God's Word by Rick Warren Copyright © 2006 by Rick Warren. Use by permission of Zondervan.

THE MINISTRY OF D-LIFE

To make disciples like Jesus, we must personally train our disciples to do the work of ministry and evangelism "outside the walls" of the church. This is an important part of living the D-Life.

Therefore, every D-Group must be committed to do the work of ministry and evangelism. We cannot disciple others through fellowship and Bible study alone. We MUST be willing to go outside the walls of the church and share in the work of ministry and evangelism together.

THE MINIMUM GOAL OF EVERY D-GROUP is to work together on **one** community ministry and evangelism project every **two** months. This means that every D-Group will participate in a minimum of **six** ministry projects each year. This is a reasonable expectation and an absolute essential for making genuine disciples.

Planning for ministry projects should be a regular part of weekly D-Group meetings. We should keep notes about ministry ideas and upcoming projects. Ministry Projects may include things such as feeding the homeless, crashing someone's yard for lawn care, doing a work project at a local school, building a wheelchair ramp, adopting a family for Christmas, prayer walk evangelism, or other creative ideas. The opportunities are endless. D-Groups can even make plans to go on a mission trip together.

The purpose for all D-Group ministry projects is servant evangelism. We want to advance God's Kingdom on earth.

Kyle Martin, with *TIME TO REVIVE* (www.timetorevive.com), teaches a simple and effective approach to servant evangelism involving the following four steps...

- **Love** – Approach an individual and engage in friendly conversation. Our main concern is to show them love. Then ask, *"Is there anything we can pray for you about?"*
- **Listen** – Listen carefully to him or her and show genuine concern.
- **Discern** – Spiritually discern how you should respond to each individual.
- **Respond** – When appropriate, pray with the individual and share the Gospel.

The *TIME TO REVIVE BIBLE* published by LIFE BIBLE STUDY (www.lifebiblestudy.com) is an excellent tool to use for sharing the Gospel. You can also use THE GOSPEL presentation on your D-Life Web App. Simply turn your mobile phone landscape and flip through the Bible verses as you present the Gospel.

USE THE SPACE BELOW TO PLAN AND KEEP A JOURNAL OF YOUR PROJECTS:

D-GROUP MINISTRY PROJECT #1
Date of Project: _____
Journal Notes on Project: _____
_____
_____
_____

D-GROUP MINISTRY PROJECT #2
Date of Project: _____
Journal Notes on Project: _____
_____
_____
_____

D-GROUP MINISTRY PROJECT #3
Date of Project: _____

Journal Notes on Project: _____

_____

_____

_____

D-GROUP MINISTRY PROJECT #4
Date of Project: _____

Journal Notes on Project: _____

_____

_____

_____

D-GROUP MINISTRY PROJECT #5
Date of Project: _____

Journal Notes on Project: _____

_____

_____

_____

D-GROUP MINISTRY PROJECT #6
Date of Project: _____

Journal Notes on Project: _____

_____

_____

_____

WEEK

Weekly Bible Reading: .... Matthew 1-5
Weekly Bible Study: .... Matthew 4:18-25

MATTHEW 1   [CIRCLE ONE: S P A C E]
Personal Study Notes: _____
_____
_____
_____

MATTHEW 2   [CIRCLE ONE: S P A C E]
Personal Study Notes: _____
_____
_____
_____

MATTHEW 3   [CIRCLE ONE: S P A C E]
Personal Study Notes: _____
_____
_____
_____

MATTHEW 4   [CIRCLE ONE: S P A C E]
Personal Study Notes: _____
_____
_____
_____

MATTHEW 5   [CIRCLE ONE: S P A C E]
Personal Study Notes: _____
_____
_____
_____

Read carefully one chapter of the Bible five days a week. In each chapter look for a . . .
Sin to Confess / **P**romise to Claim / **A**ttitude to Change / **C**ommand to Obey / **E**xample to Follow.

FISHING FOR MEN
(MATTHEW 4:18-25)

WEEKLY ASSIGNMENTS:

Lead Prayer Time: _____

Tell the Story (Paraphrase): _____

Read the Text: _____

Facilitate Bible Study: _____

DISCUSSION QUESTIONS:

- If someone wanted to go fishing today, what different tools or equipment would he or she need to take in order to catch some fish? How hard would it be to catch fish without these tools?

- In our story, Jesus is fishing for some men to be His first disciples. Who were these men and what fishing tools did they leave behind to follow Jesus? What kind of tools would Jesus begin to teach them to use to fish for people?

- Jesus said to them, "Follow me, and I will make you fishers of men" (v. 19). What do you think Jesus meant by this command? As a command for us to obey, in what ways should we be fishing for people today to become new followers of Jesus? What kind of tools can help us with this?

- Read Matt. 28:18-20. How does Jesus' first command to His followers found here in Matt. 4:19 compare to His final command in the Great Commission? In these two commands, what is Jesus saying about our purpose in life?

- As Jesus and His first disciples went throughout Galilee, what things did they observe Him doing (v. 23-24)? By proclaiming the gospel and caring for the afflicted, how was Jesus training His new followers to be "fishers of men?"

- What is the "gospel of the kingdom" (v.23) that Jesus preached? Can someone share about the time when you opened your heart to the gospel?

- As Jesus taught and cared for the people, "His fame spread" in Syria (v.24). In what ways are you helping make Jesus famous in the world today?

- As we join together in our D-Group, how will this help you become a stronger follower of Christ? How can D-Life be a tool that helps you fish for others?

PRAYER:

Let's pray today that each of us will grow stronger in our faith and better at fishing for new followers of Christ as we join together in D-Life.

PRAYER REQUESTS:

BI-MONTHLY MISSION PROJECT NOTES:

WEEK

Weekly Bible Reading: . . . . Matthew 6-10
Weekly Bible Study: . . . . Matthew 6:5-13

MATTHEW 6 [CIRCLE ONE: S P A C E]

Personal Study Notes: _____
_____
_____
_____

MATTHEW 7 [CIRCLE ONE: S P A C E]

Personal Study Notes: _____
_____
_____
_____

MATTHEW 8 [CIRCLE ONE: S P A C E]

Personal Study Notes: _____
_____
_____
_____

MATTHEW 9 [CIRCLE ONE: S P A C E]

Personal Study Notes: _____
_____
_____
_____

MATTHEW 10 [CIRCLE ONE: S P A C E]

Personal Study Notes: _____
_____
_____
_____

Read carefully one chapter of the Bible five days a week. In each chapter look for a . . .
Sin to Confess / **P**romise to Claim / **A**ttitude to Change / **C**ommand to Obey / **E**xample to Follow.

THE LORD'S PRAYER
(MATTHEW 6:5-13)

WEEKLY ASSIGNMENTS:

Lead Prayer Time: _____

Tell the Story (Paraphrase): _____

Read the Text: _____

Facilitate Bible Study: _____

DISCUSSION QUESTIONS:

- Can someone give a testimony of a time when God answered your prayer? Why is it important for us to pray?

- In our story, Jesus taught about prayer. How many times did He say, "When you pray?" Why do you think He said, "When you pray," instead of, "If you pray?"

- Where did Jesus say that "the hypocrites" liked to pray and what was their motive? What did Jesus say about their reward? What is a hypocrite?

- Where did Jesus say we should go to pray? When we do this, what did Jesus say the Father would do? Do you have a special place where you like to pray?

- Do you think it's important to pray every day? Why or why not? How much time should we spend in prayer? When is the best time for you to pray?

- Why should we not repeat meaningless phrases when we pray? Why must we pray sincere prayers from the heart instead of elegant prayers to impress others?

- What did Jesus say the Father knows about our needs even before we ask? Why is it still important for us to pray about our needs?

- In Jesus' model prayer, there is praise, intercession, petition, and confession. This is *an example to follow*. When we pray, why is it important to spend some time giving thanks and praise to God? Why should we confess our sins to God? Why should we intercede for others? Why is it important for us to pray for ourselves?

- Like daily Bible reading, prayer is a vital spiritual discipline. What did you learn from this study that can help you have a more consistent and faithful prayer life?

PRAYER:

Let's pray for one another today to be faithful in the daily spiritual discipline of prayer.

PRAYER REQUESTS:

BI-MONTHLY MISSION PROJECT NOTES:

WEEK 3

Weekly Bible Reading: . . . . Matthew 11-15
Weekly Bible Study: . . . . Matthew 13:3-9, 18-23

MATTHEW 11 [CIRCLE ONE: S P A C E]

Personal Study Notes: _____

_____

_____

_____

MATTHEW 12 [CIRCLE ONE: S P A C E]

Personal Study Notes: _____

_____

_____

_____

MATTHEW 13 [CIRCLE ONE: S P A C E]

Personal Study Notes: _____

_____

_____

_____

MATTHEW 14 [CIRCLE ONE: S P A C E]

Personal Study Notes: _____

_____

_____

_____

MATTHEW 15 [CIRCLE ONE: S P A C E]

Personal Study Notes: _____

_____

_____

_____

Read carefully one chapter of the Bible five days a week. In each chapter look for a . . .
Sin to Confess / **P**romise to Claim / **A**ttitude to Change / **C**ommand to Obey / **E**xample to Follow.

THE SOWER AND THE SEED
(MATTHEW 13:3-9, 18-23)

WEEKLY ASSIGNMENTS:

Lead Prayer Time: _____

Tell the Story (Paraphrase): _____

Read the Text: _____

Facilitate Bible Study: _____

DISCUSSION QUESTIONS:

- Have you ever tried to grow anything? If so, what did you try to grow and how are your gardening skills? What have you learned about gardening?

- In our story, Jesus told a story about gardening and explained its meaning. Who did "the sower" represent and what is "the seed" that he was sowing? What did the different types of soil represent?

- Who did the birds represent and what did they do to the seeds that fell by the wayside? It what ways does "the evil one" snatch away the Gospel seed?

- Why do you think some people develop a hard heart toward God and the good news of the Gospel? What are the best ways to share our faith with people who are hardened toward God and the Gospel?

- What did the rocky soil represent? What two things did Jesus say reveal a shallow commitment to Christ? What happens to the seed in this soil?

- What did the thorny soil represent? What two things did Jesus say reveal an uncertain commitment to Christ? What happens to the seed in this soil?

- What did the good soil represent? What is the one thing that reveals a true commitment to Christ? What is spiritual fruit? Do all true believers bear spiritual fruit? Why do you think some believers bear more fruit than others?

- In what way is the sower an example to follow? Even though everyone will not be receptive, why is it important for us to continually share our faith?

- Which of the soils in this story do you most identify with and why? In what ways can your life become more fruitful for God?

PRAYER:

Let's pray for one another today that our lives will bear much fruit for God.

PRAYER REQUESTS:

BI-MONTHLY MISSION PROJECT NOTES:

WEEK

Weekly Bible Reading: .... Matthew 16-20
Weekly Bible Study: .... Matthew 18:21-35

MATTHEW 16   [CIRCLE ONE: S P A C E]

Personal Study Notes: _____

_____

_____

_____

MATTHEW 17   [CIRCLE ONE: S P A C E]

Personal Study Notes: _____

_____

_____

_____

MATTHEW 18   [CIRCLE ONE: S P A C E]

Personal Study Notes: _____

_____

_____

_____

MATTHEW 19   [CIRCLE ONE: S P A C E]

Personal Study Notes: _____

_____

_____

_____

MATTHEW 20   [CIRCLE ONE: S P A C E]

Personal Study Notes: _____

_____

_____

_____

Read carefully one chapter of the Bible five days a week. In each chapter look for a . . .
Sin to Confess / **P**romise to Claim / **A**ttitude to Change / **C**ommand to Obey / **E**xample to Follow.

THE UNFORGIVING SERVANT
(MATTHEW 18:21-35)

WEEKLY ASSIGNMENTS:

Lead Prayer Time: _____

Tell the Story (Paraphrase): _____

Read the Text: _____

Facilitate Bible Study: _____

DISCUSSION QUESTIONS:

- Why is it a bad thing to be in debt to someone? How does it make you feel when you are able to pay off a debt?

- In our story, we read about a certain king who wished to settle accounts with his servants. Who do you think the king represents? Who do his servants represent?

- How much debt did the first servant owe to the king? What was significant about this amount of debt? Since the servant was too poor to pay the debt, what did the king demand from him?

- How did the servant respond to the king's demands and what did he beg of the king? What was the king's response to the servant's pleas? In what ways can we relate the king's merciful response to our own relationship with God?

- What happened after the forgiven servant left the king's presence? How much did his fellow servant owe to him? What is significant about this amount in comparison to the previous amount owed to the king?

- What was the man's reply to his fellow servant's pleas for mercy? When others witnessed the man's unwillingness to forgive, how did they feel about it? Who did they tell about it? How did the king respond to this news?

- How does God feel about us when we are unwilling to forgive others? What did Jesus mean when He said we are to forgive others from the heart? When we forgive someone a debt does that person still owe us anything?

- In what ways can we see in this story a *sin to confess or an attitude to change*? Is there anyone that you need to forgive today? What will you do about it?

PRAYER:

Let's thank God today that we are His forgiven servants, and pray that God will give us a spirit of forgiveness toward those who have offended us.

PRAYER REQUESTS:

BI-MONTHLY MISSION PROJECT NOTES:

WEEK

MATTHEW 21 [CIRCLE ONE: S P A C E]
Personal Study Notes: _____

_____

_____

_____

MATTHEW 22 [CIRCLE ONE: S P A C E]
Personal Study Notes: _____

_____

_____

_____

MATTHEW 23 [CIRCLE ONE: S P A C E]
Personal Study Notes: _____

_____

_____

_____

MATTHEW 24 [CIRCLE ONE: S P A C E]
Personal Study Notes: _____

_____

_____

_____

MATTHEW 25 [CIRCLE ONE: S P A C E]
Personal Study Notes: _____

_____

_____

_____

Read carefully one chapter of the Bible five days a week. In each chapter look for a . . .
Sin to Confess / **P**romise to Claim / **A**ttitude to Change / **C**ommand to Obey / **E**xample to Follow.

THE STORY OF THE TALENTS
(MATTHEW 25:14-30)

WEEKLY ASSIGNMENTS:

Lead Prayer Time: _____

Tell the Story (Paraphrase): _____

Read the Text: _____

Facilitate Bible Study: _____

DISCUSSION QUESTIONS:

- Just for fun, if you could have any special talent in the world, what would it be? How would you use this talent if you had it?

- In our story, Jesus told about a man going on a journey who gave certain "talents" to his servants. Who do you think this man represents? Who do the servants represent? What do the talents represent?

- Why do you think this man gave a different amount of talents to each of his servants? Regardless of the amount of their talents, what do you think the man expected the servants to do with their talents?

- What did the five-talent servant do with his talents? What did the two-talent servant do with his talents? What did the one-talent servant do?

- When the master returned, what did he say to the two servants who had used their talents wisely? How do you think this made them feel?

- What excuse did the one-talent servant give for his actions? Does his excuse make any sense? What did the master call this servant? What did the master do to this servant? How might this servant's actions be a sin to confess?

- What God-given talents or gifts do you have? In what ways are you currently using your talents and spiritual gifts for the Lord?

- When we are faithful to God with the little things He has given us, what did God say He would do? When we are unfaithful with what God has given us, what will He do? What does it mean "to enter into the joy of your Lord?"

- If Jesus were to return today, do you think you would hear Him say, "Well done My good and faithful servant?" Why or why not?

PRAYER:

Let's thank God today for the talents He has given us and pray that we will use them wisely for His glory.

PRAYER REQUESTS:

BI-MONTHLY MISSION PROJECT NOTES:

WEEK 6

Weekly Bible Reading: .... Matthew 26-Mark 2
Weekly Bible Study: .... Matthew 28:16-20

MATTHEW 26   [CIRCLE ONE: S P A C E]

Personal Study Notes: _____

_____

_____

_____

MATTHEW 27   [CIRCLE ONE: S P A C E]

Personal Study Notes: _____

_____

_____

_____

MATTHEW 28   [CIRCLE ONE: S P A C E]

Personal Study Notes: _____

_____

_____

_____

MARK 1   [CIRCLE ONE: S P A C E]

Personal Study Notes: _____

_____

_____

_____

MARK 2   [CIRCLE ONE: S P A C E]

Personal Study Notes: _____

_____

_____

_____

Read carefully one chapter of the Bible five days a week. In each chapter look for a . . .
Sin to Confess / **P**romise to Claim / **A**ttitude to Change / **C**ommand to Obey / **E**xample to Follow.

THE GREAT COMMISSION
(MATTHEW 28:16-20)

WEEKLY ASSIGNMENTS:

Lead Prayer Time: _____

Tell the Story (Paraphrase): _____

Read the Text: _____

Facilitate Bible Study: _____

DISCUSSION QUESTIONS:

- Why do you think people like to go to the mountains; what is so special about a mountain? What mountains do you like to visit and what special memories do you have from your visits there?

- In our story, the resurrected Jesus instructed His disciples to go to a mountain for some time alone with Him. Jesus seemed to like mountains. What other significant events in Jesus' life took place on mountains?

- What did the eleven disciples do when they saw Jesus on the mountain? Who do you think might have been the ones who doubted?

- How much authority did Jesus say He had been given? Why do you think Jesus acknowledged His authority before giving His Great Commission?

- Why are Jesus' final words to His followers called the Great Commission? Do you think this is a suggestion to consider or a command to obey? Why do you think this? Why do you think many treat it as a suggestion?

- In the Great Commission, what one main thing did the resurrected Jesus commanded His followers to do? How is "making disciples" different from "making converts?" Where are we called to make disciples?

- Jesus instructed that new disciples should be baptized and then they should be taught (v. 20-21). What did Jesus say new disciples should be taught? How is the principle of discipleship multiplication conveyed in Jesus' instructions?

- What did Jesus say He would do for all who go to make and multiply disciples? In what ways are you personally involved in fulfilling the Great Commission? In what ways is your D-Group helping you with this?

PRAYER:

Let's pray today that we will continue to grow as followers of Jesus and become disciples who make other disciples.

PRAYER REQUESTS:

BI-MONTHLY MISSION PROJECT NOTES:

WEEK

Weekly Bible Reading: .... Mark 3-7
Weekly Bible Study: .... Mark 5:1-20

MARK 3   [CIRCLE ONE: S P A C E]
*Personal Study Notes:*_____

_____

_____

_____

MARK 4   [CIRCLE ONE: S P A C E]
*Personal Study Notes:*_____

_____

_____

_____

MARK 5   [CIRCLE ONE: S P A C E]
*Personal Study Notes:*_____

_____

_____

_____

MARK 6   [CIRCLE ONE: S P A C E]
*Personal Study Notes:*_____

_____

_____

_____

MARK 7   [CIRCLE ONE: S P A C E]
*Personal Study Notes:*_____

_____

_____

_____

Read carefully one chapter of the Bible five days a week. In each chapter look for a . . .
Sin to Confess / **P**romise to Claim / **A**ttitude to Change / **C**ommand to Obey / **E**xample to Follow.

A MAN WITH AN UNCLEAN SPIRIT
(MARK 5:1-20)

WEEKLY ASSIGNMENTS:

Lead Prayer Time: _____

Tell the Story (Paraphrase): _____

Read the Text: _____

Facilitate Bible Study: _____

DISCUSSION QUESTIONS:

- Who is the meanest person you have ever known? What do you think made this person so mean? How did this person affect your life?

- In our story, we are told about a man with an unclean spirit. What is an unclean spirit? What power did the unclean spirit have over this man's life? Why do you think this man lived among the tombs?

- What did the man with the unclean spirit do when he saw Jesus? How do you think he was able to do this? Why do you think he did this?

- What did the unclean spirit know about Jesus that many people did not know? What did the unclean spirit ask Jesus not to do to him? What was the spirit's name and what did his name mean?

- Why do you think Jesus allowed the unclean spirits to go into the swine? What happened to those demon possessed swine? What lesson can we learn from this about Satan and his demons?

- How is the man described after he was set free from the unclean spirit? What does this teach us about the power of Jesus to change lives? What do you believe about "unclean spirits" and demon possession today?

- Perhaps we all battle with demons more than we realize. Are there any particular demons you've been battling with lately? How can we help?

- What did this man do after Jesus saved him? How is this *an example for us to follow*? What are some of the great things Jesus has done for you?

PRAYER:

Let's pray that God will give us the opportunity today to share with others about the great things that Jesus has done for us.

PRAYER REQUESTS:

BI-MONTHLY MISSION PROJECT NOTES:

WEEK 8

Weekly Bible Reading: .... Mark 8-12
Weekly Bible Study: .... Mark 10:35-45

MARK 8
[CIRCLE ONE: S P A C E]

Personal Study Notes: _____

_____

_____

_____

MARK 9
[CIRCLE ONE: S P A C E]

Personal Study Notes: _____

_____

_____

_____

MARK 10
[CIRCLE ONE: S P A C E]

Personal Study Notes: _____

_____

_____

_____

MARK 11
[CIRCLE ONE: S P A C E]

Personal Study Notes: _____

_____

_____

_____

MARK 12
[CIRCLE ONE: S P A C E]

Personal Study Notes: _____

_____

_____

_____

Read carefully one chapter of the Bible five days a week. In each chapter look for a . . .
Sin to Confess / **P**romise to Claim / **A**ttitude to Change / **C**ommand to Obey / **E**xample to Follow.

JESUS TEACHES ON BEING A SERVANT
(MARK 10:35-45)

WEEKLY ASSIGNMENTS:

Lead Prayer Time: _____

Tell the Story (Paraphrase): _____

Read the Text: _____

Facilitate Bible Study: _____

DISCUSSION QUESTIONS:

- Who would you consider to be the greatest person you have ever met? What made this person great and how did it make you feel to meet him or her?

- In our story, James and John came to Jesus with a selfish request and Jesus used the occasion to teach on being a servant. What did they request of Jesus? Do you think they knew what they were asking? Why or why not?

- In Jesus' response to James and John, what specific question did He ask them? What kind of "cup" and "baptism" do you think Jesus is referring to?

- How did James and John answer Jesus' question? Why did Jesus say that He could not grant their request?

- How did the other disciples feel about all this? Why do you think they felt this way? What made this a good time for

Jesus to teach on being a servant?

- What did Jesus say about the leadership practices of the "Gentiles" or worldly rulers? How does it make you feel when someone "lords over you?"

- In what way did Jesus say that His disciples must be different from worldly rulers? What does it mean to be a servant-leader? What makes a servant-leader better than an authoritative leader?

- What did Jesus say a person must do to be truly great? In what ways did Jesus model this? How is this an *attitude* to change about greatness?

- Why do you think Jesus often referred to Himself as the "Son of Man" instead of the "Son of God?" What did He say that the "Son of Man" came to do? What does it mean that Jesus gave His life "as a ransom for many?"

- In what ways are you a servant-leader? If you are not serving God and others what does this say about you? What is one way that you could become a better servant and a truly "greater" person?

PRAYER:

Let's pray that God will give us the opportunity today to share with others about the great things that Jesus has done for us.

PRAYER REQUESTS:

BI-MONTHLY MISSION PROJECT NOTES:

WEEK

Weekly Bible Reading: .... Mark 13 – Luke 1
Weekly Bible Study: .... Mark 14:1-9

MARK 13
[CIRCLE ONE: S P A C E]
*Personal Study Notes:*_____
_____
_____
_____

MARK 14
[CIRCLE ONE: S P A C E]
*Personal Study Notes:*_____
_____
_____
_____

MARK 15
[CIRCLE ONE: S P A C E]
*Personal Study Notes:*_____
_____
_____
_____

MARK 16
[CIRCLE ONE: S P A C E]
*Personal Study Notes:*_____
_____
_____
_____

LUKE 1
[CIRCLE ONE: S P A C E]
*Personal Study Notes:*_____
_____
_____
_____

Read carefully one chapter of the Bible five days a week. In each chapter look for a . . .
Sin to Confess / **P**romise to Claim / **A**ttitude to Change / **C**ommand to Obey / **E**xample to Follow.

THE ANOINTING OF JESUS AT BETHANY
(MARK 14:1-9)

WEEKLY ASSIGNMENTS:

Lead Prayer Time: _____

Tell the Story (Paraphrase): _____

Read the Text: _____

Facilitate Bible Study: _____

DISCUSSION QUESTIONS:

- What is the most extravagant gift anyone has ever given you? How did it make you feel to receive this gift?

- In our story, a woman gave Jesus a very extravagant gift. According to Mark, when did this story happen? What was significant about "the Passover" to the Jewish people? What were the chief priests and scribes plotting to do?

- According to Mark, where did this story occur? What miracle had Jesus likely performed for the owner of the house where Jesus was staying?

- Read John 12:1-3. If John is sharing about this same story, who were other guests in the house? According to John, who was the woman that anointed Jesus with her costly ointment? What did she do with her hair?

- Why do you think this woman gave Jesus such an extravagant expression of love and worship? What part might her gratitude toward Jesus have played in this? How do you think it made Jesus feel to receive this gift?

- Why do you think some people were critical of her? What question did her critics raise about her actions? How did Jesus respond to her critics?

- Do you think this woman was one of the few people who truly understood the sacrifice Jesus was about to make? Why or why not? What did Jesus say would be true about this woman?

- How are the actions of this woman *an example for us to follow*? How is the attitude of her critics *an attitude we might need to change*?

- Of all the characters involved in this story, who do you most identify with and why? How does your worship of Jesus compare to that of the woman's? How might your worship be different as a result our study of this story?

PRAYER:

Let's pray that God will give us a heart of unreserved worship for Jesus.

PRAYER REQUESTS:

BI-MONTHLY MISSION PROJECT NOTES:

WEEK

Weekly Bible Reading: . . . . Luke 2-6
Weekly Bible Study: . . . . Luke 4:1-13

LUKE 2
[CIRCLE ONE: S P A C E]

Personal Study Notes: _____

_____

_____

_____

LUKE 3
[CIRCLE ONE: S P A C E]

Personal Study Notes: _____

_____

_____

_____

LUKE 4
[CIRCLE ONE: S P A C E]

Personal Study Notes: _____

_____

_____

_____

LUKE 5
[CIRCLE ONE: S P A C E]

Personal Study Notes: _____

_____

_____

_____

LUKE 6
[CIRCLE ONE: S P A C E]

Personal Study Notes: _____

_____

_____

_____

Read carefully one chapter of the Bible five days a week. In each chapter look for a . . .
Sin to Confess / **P**romise to Claim / **A**ttitude to Change / **C**ommand to Obey / **E**xample to Follow.

THE TEMPTATION OF JESUS
(LUKE 4:1-13)

WEEKLY ASSIGNMENTS:

Lead Prayer Time: _____

Tell the Story (Paraphrase): _____

Read the Text: _____

Facilitate Bible Study: _____

DISCUSSION QUESTIONS:

- How does it make you feel when you are extremely hungry? What is your attitude like when you go without food?

- In our story, the Holy Spirit led Jesus into the wilderness for forty days to fast and pray. How do you think Jesus must have felt after going forty days without any food? What is the longest that you have ever fasted? How did it make you feel physically? What did it do for you spiritually?

- Who is the devil and what is his purpose? Do you believe he is real? Why or why not? Read John 8:44. In this verse, what did Jesus say about the devil?

- Why do you think the devil chose this occasion as a time of temptation for Jesus? What is temptation? How does the devil tempt us? How often does he tempt us to sin? Is it a sin to be tempted? Why or why not?

- In the devil's first two temptations, in what ways did he try to appeal to Jesus in the areas of flesh and pride? In what ways does he try to tempt us with sins of the flesh? In what ways does he try to tempt us with sins of pride?

- What was unique about the devil's third temptation of Jesus? What important lesson can we learn from this about the devil?

- In all three temptations, how did Jesus respond? As an *example to follow*, what can we learn from Jesus about resisting temptation? Read James 4:7. What does this verse teach us? What happens when we fall to temptation?

- From Jesus' example, why is daily Bible reading and Bible study a vital part of overcoming temptation? According to Luke, how long did the devil "depart from Jesus?" When will we ever stop having to deal with temptation?

- What particular area of temptation has the devil been attacking you with lately? How are you holding up to this attack? Are there any specific ways we can help you resist the devil and his temptation?

PRAYER:

Let's pray today that the Lord will lead us not into temptation, but that He will deliver us from all evil.

PRAYER REQUESTS:

BI-MONTHLY MISSION PROJECT NOTES:

WEEK 11

Weekly Bible Reading: .... Luke 7-11
Weekly Bible Study: .... Luke 10:25-37

LUKE 7
[CIRCLE ONE: S P A C E]

Personal Study Notes: _____

_____

_____

_____

LUKE 8
[CIRCLE ONE: S P A C E]

Personal Study Notes: _____

_____

_____

_____

LUKE 9
[CIRCLE ONE: S P A C E]

Personal Study Notes: _____

_____

_____

_____

LUKE 10
[CIRCLE ONE: S P A C E]

Personal Study Notes: _____

_____

_____

_____

LUKE 11
[CIRCLE ONE: S P A C E]

Personal Study Notes: _____

_____

_____

_____

Read carefully one chapter of the Bible five days a week. In each chapter look for a . . .
Sin to Confess / **P**romise to Claim / **A**ttitude to Change / **C**ommand to Obey / **E**xample to Follow.

THE GOOD SAMARITAN
(LUKE 10:25-37)

WEEKLY ASSIGNMENTS:

Lead Prayer Time: _____

Tell the Story (Paraphrase): _____

Read the Text: _____

Facilitate Bible Study: _____

DISCUSSION QUESTIONS:

- When is the last time you helped someone in a difficult situation? What did you do for the person and how did it make you feel?

- In our story, Jesus told about a Good Samaritan who helped someone in a difficult situation. With whom was Jesus speaking and what led Him to tell this story? Why do you think Jesus often responded to a person's question by telling a story?

- Who were the Samaritans? How did Jews and Samaritans feel about one another? Why did they feel this way?

- In Jesus' story, what happened to the "certain man" who went down from Jerusalem to Jericho? What difficult situation did he find himself in?

- Who were the first two people who came across the man? What is significant about the professions of these two men? How did they respond to the man's need? Why do you think they responded this way?

- Who was the third person to come across the man? What is significant about his race? What did he feel in his heart toward this man? How did he respond to the man's need? What did it cost him? In what ways are the actions of the Good Samaritan an example for us to follow?

- What does this story teach us about being a neighbor? What does it teach us about religious hypocrisy? What does it teach us about prejudice?

- In many ways, Jesus was the ultimate "Good Samaritan." In what ways are we like the man who fell among thieves? In what ways is Jesus like the Good Samaritan to us?

- The next time you come across a stranger in need, how will this story effect the way your respond?

PRAYER:

Let's pray today that God will give us a greater heart of compassion for people in need so that we can show them the love of Christ.

PRAYER REQUESTS:

BI-MONTHLY MISSION PROJECT NOTES:

WEEK 12

Weekly Bible Reading: . . . . Luke 12-16
Weekly Bible Study: . . . . Luke 15:11-32

LUKE 12   [CIRCLE ONE: S P A C E]
Personal Study Notes: _____

_____

_____

_____

LUKE 13   [CIRCLE ONE: S P A C E]
Personal Study Notes: _____

_____

_____

_____

LUKE 14   [CIRCLE ONE: S P A C E]
Personal Study Notes: _____

_____

_____

_____

LUKE 15   [CIRCLE ONE: S P A C E]
Personal Study Notes: _____

_____

_____

_____

LUKE 16   [CIRCLE ONE: S P A C E]
Personal Study Notes: _____

_____

_____

_____

Read carefully one chapter of the Bible five days a week. In each chapter look for a . . .
Sin to Confess / **P**romise to Claim / **A**ttitude to Change / **C**ommand to Obey / **E**xample to Follow.

THE PRODIGAL SON
(LUKE 15:11-32)

WEEKLY ASSIGNMENTS:

Lead Prayer Time: _____

Tell the Story (Paraphrase): _____

Read the Text: _____

Facilitate Bible Study: _____

DISCUSSION QUESTIONS:

- What is a rebel? Have you ever been rebellious and, if so, when and why?

- In our story, Jesus told about a father and his two sons. Who do you think the father represents? Who does the younger brother represent? Who does the older brother represent? What does the far away country represent?

- What did the younger son ask of his father? Why do you think the father granted his request? How do you think the father felt about this?

- After receiving his inheritance, where did the younger son go? What did he do there? After spending up all he had, what happened in the country where he was? What lowly job did he do to try to survive in the far away country?

- How was he treated by the citizens of this country? Do you think his new company of friends really cared for him? Why or why not?

- After tending to the pigs and coveting their food, what finally happened to the younger son's attitude? What were his thoughts about his father?

- How did the father respond to his son's return? What does this story teach us about the Heavenly Father's great love for us?

- How did the older brother respond to his brother's return? In what ways do we see in the older brother an *attitude to change*?

- When the younger son was far from his father and in desperate need, the Bible says, "he came to himself" (v. 17). What do you think this means? Can you describe a "come to yourself" experience in your own spiritual life?

- Why do some people think that living far away from the Father is better than living with Him? What do you think about this? Who do you most identify with in this story and why?

PRAYER:

Let's pray today for someone we know who is living far away from God.

PRAYER REQUESTS:

BI-MONTHLY MISSION PROJECT NOTES:

WEEK 13

Weekly Bible Reading: .... Luke 17-21
Weekly Bible Study: .... Luke 18:1-8

LUKE 17   [CIRCLE ONE: S P A C E]
*Personal Study Notes:*_____

_____

_____

_____

LUKE 18   [CIRCLE ONE: S P A C E]
*Personal Study Notes:*_____

_____

_____

_____

LUKE 19   [CIRCLE ONE: S P A C E]
*Personal Study Notes:*_____

_____

_____

_____

LUKE 20   [CIRCLE ONE: S P A C E]
*Personal Study Notes:*_____

_____

_____

_____

LUKE 21   [CIRCLE ONE: S P A C E]
*Personal Study Notes:*_____

_____

_____

_____

Read carefully one chapter of the Bible five days a week. In each chapter look for a . . .
Sin to Confess / **P**romise to Claim / **A**ttitude to Change / **C**ommand to Obey / **E**xample to Follow.

THE PERSISTENT WIDOW
(LUKE 18:1-8)

WEEKLY ASSIGNMENTS:

Lead Prayer Time: _____

Tell the Story (Paraphrase): _____

Read the Text: _____

Facilitate Bible Study: _____

DISCUSSION QUESTIONS:

- How is your prayer life? What do you find most challenging about prayer?

- In our story, Jesus shared a story about a widow who was very persistent in her request for justice. According to Luke, for what specific reason did Jesus tell this story? How does prayer keep us from losing heart?

- What kind of person was the judge in this story? What was the widow's request that she brought before the judge? How did he respond at first?

- What did the widow do when the judge did not grant her request? How did the judge respond to her persistence?

- How does it make you feel when God does not seem to answer your prayers? What lesson do we learn about prayer from this persistent woman? In what ways are her actions *an example to follow*?

- How is God different from the irreverent judge in this story? What will God do for his elect who cry out to Him day and night?

- What did Jesus mean by saying, "When the Son of Man comes, will He really find faith on the earth?" What does the widow woman's persistence in prayer indicate about her faith?

- What is your greatest prayer burden today? Can you give a personal testimony of how God answered your persistent prayer over a burden in your own life?

PRAYER:

Let's pray today that God will give us the faith to pray with persistence over the burdens of our hearts.

PRAYER REQUESTS:

BI-MONTHLY MISSION PROJECT NOTES:

WEEK 14

LUKE 22   [CIRCLE ONE: S P A C E]

Personal Study Notes: _____

_____

_____

_____

LUKE 23   [CIRCLE ONE: S P A C E]

Personal Study Notes: _____

_____

_____

_____

LUKE 24   [CIRCLE ONE: S P A C E]

Personal Study Notes: _____

_____

_____

_____

JOHN 1   [CIRCLE ONE: S P A C E]

Personal Study Notes: _____

_____

_____

_____

JOHN 2   [CIRCLE ONE: S P A C E]

Personal Study Notes: _____

_____

_____

_____

Read carefully one chapter of the Bible five days a week. In each chapter look for a . . .
Sin to Confess / **P**romise to Claim / **A**ttitude to Change / **C**ommand to Obey / **E**xample to Follow.

THE ROAD TO EMMAUS
(LUKE 24:13-35)

WEEKLY ASSIGNMENTS:

Lead Prayer Time: _____

Tell the Story (Paraphrase): _____

Read the Text: _____

Facilitate Bible Study: _____

DISCUSSION QUESTIONS:

- What is the biggest news event that has occurred in your lifetime? Where were you when you first heard about this news?

- In our story, two travelers were walking to the village of Emmaus while discussing some big news that had just happened in Jerusalem. Who were these two travelers on the road to Emmaus? How far was Emmaus from Jerusalem? What big news had just happened In Jerusalem?

- Who was the third person that joined in their conversation? Why were the two travelers surprised by "the stranger's" question? What things did they describe for the man about the events that had just happened in Jerusalem?

- What amazing news did the travelers say was reported by some women who had visited Jesus' tomb? How did people respond to the women's report?

- What was "the stranger's" response to these two travelers? What does it mean to be "slow of heart to believe?" In what ways is being slow of heart to believe *an attitude to change*?

- What do you think might have been some of the Scriptures that Jesus used to share with these travelers concerning Himself? Read Isaiah 53:3-6. How might Jesus have used these Scriptures to instruct them concerning Himself?

- When did the travelers recognize that the man with them was Jesus? How did the travelers describe their Emmaus Road experience?

- Is your heart cold, lukewarm, or burning hot for the Word of God? Are you slow to believe or quick to believe the promises of God? What would help you to hunger more for God's word? What would help you to grow in faith?

- What does it mean to you today that Jesus has risen from the dead?

PRAYER:

Let's pray for one another today, that we will walk so closely with Jesus that our hearts will burn with passion for His Word and that our faith will grow.

PRAYER REQUESTS:

BI-MONTHLY MISSION PROJECT NOTES:

WEEK 15

Weekly Bible Reading: .... John 3-7
Weekly Bible Study: .... John 3:1-16

JOHN 3 [CIRCLE ONE: S P A C E]
Personal Study Notes: _____
_____
_____
_____

JOHN 4 [CIRCLE ONE: S P A C E]
Personal Study Notes: _____
_____
_____
_____

JOHN 5 [CIRCLE ONE: S P A C E]
Personal Study Notes: _____
_____
_____
_____

JOHN 6 [CIRCLE ONE: S P A C E]
Personal Study Notes: _____
_____
_____
_____

JOHN 7 [CIRCLE ONE: S P A C E]
Personal Study Notes: _____
_____
_____
_____

Read carefully one chapter of the Bible five days a week. In each chapter look for a . . .
Sin to Confess / **P**romise to Claim / **A**ttitude to Change / **C**ommand to Obey / **E**xample to Follow.

NICODEMUS COMES TO JESUS
(JOHN 3:1-16)

WEEKLY ASSIGNMENTS:

Lead Prayer Time: _____

Tell the Story (Paraphrase): _____

Read the Text: _____

Facilitate Bible Study: _____

DISCUSSION QUESTIONS:

- Where is the most unusual place you have seen "John 3:16?" Why do you think this verse is so famous?

- In our story, a Pharisee named Nicodemus came to Jesus and Jesus told him that he must be born again. Who were the Pharisees? Why do you think Nicodemus came to Jesus "by night?" Who did he say that Jesus was?

- What do you think Jesus meant when he told Nicodemus that he "must be born again?" In what way did Nicodemus misunderstand Jesus? What did Jesus say a person cannot do unless he or she is "born again?"

- What do you think it means to be born of water and of the Spirit? What illustration from nature did Jesus use to explain spiritual birth? How does this illustration help you understand spiritual birth?

- What did Jesus mean by telling Nicodemus that He had "descended from heaven?" Why do you think Jesus referred to Himself as "the Son of Man?"

- Read Numbers 21:4-9. In what ways does the story of Moses lifting up the serpent in the wilderness compare to Jesus being lifted up on the cross? Do you think Nicodemus was ever born again? Why or why not?

- In John 3:16, how much did Jesus say that God loved the whole world? What must everyone in the world do to have everlasting life? Do you think there are other ways for people to be saved? Why or why not?

- Can you share about the time when you were "born again?" What evidences of spiritual birth can be seen in your life? Why is it important for you to share with others how they can be born again?

PRAYER:

Let's pray today that God will give us opportunities to have meaningful conversations with others about being born again.

PRAYER REQUESTS:

BI-MONTHLY MISSION PROJECT NOTES:

WEEK 16

Weekly Bible Reading: .... John 8-12
Weekly Bible Study: .... John 11:1-44

JOHN 8   [CIRCLE ONE: S P A C E]
Personal Study Notes: _____

_____

_____

_____

JOHN 9   [CIRCLE ONE: S P A C E]
Personal Study Notes: _____

_____

_____

_____

JOHN 10   [CIRCLE ONE: S P A C E]
Personal Study Notes: _____

_____

_____

_____

JOHN 11   [CIRCLE ONE: S P A C E]
Personal Study Notes: _____

_____

_____

_____

JOHN 12   [CIRCLE ONE: S P A C E]
Personal Study Notes: _____

_____

_____

_____

Read carefully one chapter of the Bible five days a week. In each chapter look for a . . .
Sin to Confess / **P**romise to Claim / **A**ttitude to Change / **C**ommand to Obey / **E**xample to Follow.

JESUS RAISES LAZARUS
(JOHN 11:1-44)

WEEKLY ASSIGNMENTS:

Lead Prayer Time: _____

Tell the Story (Paraphrase): _____

Read the Text: _____

Facilitate Bible Study: _____

DISCUSSION QUESTIONS:

- If someone that you love was suffering with a fatal illness, how would it make you feel? What would you want to do for him or her?

- In our story, Lazarus, the brother of Martha and Mary, was suffering with a fatal illness. What important thing did Martha and Mary do for their sick brother? Why is it important for us to pray for those who are sick?

- What did Jesus say about Lazarus' sickness? What do you think He meant by this? How long did Jesus wait before He went to Lazarus? Why do you think He delayed? When God delays to answer prayer, what is He teaching us?

- Why were the disciples concerned about going back to Judea? How did Jesus respond to their concern? Why did Jesus say He was "glad" that Lazarus had died? Which disciple spoke up and what leadership did he show?

- When Jesus arrived in Bethany, how long had Lazarus been in the tomb? What did both Martha and Mary say to Jesus and what do you think they were implying by their words? Why do you think "Jesus wept?"

- What powerful "I AM" statement did Jesus share with Martha and what does this mean? What amazing thing did Jesus say was true for all who believe in Him? How does this wonderful promise to claim effect your life?

- What question did Jesus ask Martha and what was her response? How would you respond to this question? What did it prove when Jesus raised Lazarus?

- Knowing that Jesus is the Resurrection and the Life, how does this change the way you pray? How does this give you hope in difficult times? How does this help you deal with death and grief? How does this make you want to share Jesus with others? Who is someone you need to share Jesus with soon?

PRAYER:

Let's pray today that God will give us an opportunity very soon to share with a friend about the One who is the Resurrection and the Life.

PRAYER REQUESTS:

BI-MONTHLY MISSION PROJECT NOTES:

WEEK 17

JOHN 13   [CIRCLE ONE: S P A C E]

Personal Study Notes: _____

_____

_____

_____

JOHN 14   [CIRCLE ONE: S P A C E]

Personal Study Notes: _____

_____

_____

_____

JOHN 15   [CIRCLE ONE: S P A C E]

Personal Study Notes: _____

_____

_____

_____

JOHN 16   [CIRCLE ONE: S P A C E]

Personal Study Notes: _____

_____

_____

_____

JOHN 17   [CIRCLE ONE: S P A C E]

Personal Study Notes: _____

_____

_____

_____

Read carefully one chapter of the Bible five days a week. In each chapter look for a . . .
Sin to Confess / **P**romise to Claim / **A**ttitude to Change / **C**ommand to Obey / **E**xample to Follow.

JESUS WASHES THE DISCIPLES' FEET
(JOHN 13:1-15)

WEEKLY ASSIGNMENTS:

Lead Prayer Time: _____

Tell the Story (Paraphrase): _____

Read the Text: _____

Facilitate Bible Study: _____

DISCUSSION QUESTIONS:

- What is the most humble act of service you have ever done? How did it make you feel to serve someone in this way?

- In our story, Jesus and His disciples shared their last Passover meal together. What was the Feast of the Passover? What did Jesus know about Himself at this particular Passover? What business was the Devil up to at this Passover? Did Judas have to betray Jesus or was it his choice?

- Where did John say that Jesus had come from and where was He going? What did John say that the Father had given to Jesus and what did He mean by this?

- Why do you think Jesus washed the dirty feet of His disciples? This being Jesus' last meal with the disciples, what main lesson do you think He wanted to leave with them?

- How do you think you would have felt if you were one of the disciples and Jesus was about to wash your feet? How did Peter feel about Jesus washing his feet? What did Jesus say to Peter and what did He mean by this?

- When Jesus said, "He who is bathed needs only to wash his feet, but is completely clean," what do you think He was saying? Who do you think Jesus was referring to when He told the disciples that not all of them were clean?

- After washing the disciples' feet, what *command* to obey did Jesus give? What are some practical ways that you can follow Jesus' example and obey this command? Figuratively speaking, can you share a testimony of a time when someone has "washed your feet?"

- In what ways can our D-Group follow Jesus' example through our bi-monthly ministry and evangelism projects?

PRAYER:

Let's pray today that God will give each of us an opportunity this week to wash someone's feet.

PRAYER REQUESTS:

BI-MONTHLY MISSION PROJECT NOTES:

WEEK 18

Weekly Bible Reading: .... John 18 – Acts 1
Weekly Bible Study: .... John 21:3-17

JOHN 18   [CIRCLE ONE: S P A C E]
Personal Study Notes: _____
_____
_____
_____

JOHN 19   [CIRCLE ONE: S P A C E]
Personal Study Notes: _____
_____
_____
_____

JOHN 20   [CIRCLE ONE: S P A C E]
Personal Study Notes: _____
_____
_____
_____

JOHN 21   [CIRCLE ONE: S P A C E]
Personal Study Notes: _____
_____
_____
_____

ACTS 1   [CIRCLE ONE: S P A C E]
Personal Study Notes: _____
_____
_____
_____

Read carefully one chapter of the Bible five days a week. In each chapter look for a . . .
Sin to Confess / **P**romise to Claim / **A**ttitude to Change / **C**ommand to Obey / **E**xample to Follow.

FEED MY SHEEP
(JOHN 21:3-17)

WEEKLY ASSIGNMENTS:

Lead Prayer Time: _____

Tell the Story (Paraphrase): _____

Read the Text: _____

Facilitate Bible Study: _____

DISCUSSION QUESTIONS:

- Have you ever let someone down who was counting on you? When did this happen and how did it make you feel?

- In our story, Simon Peter had let Jesus down by denying Him three times, but Jesus found him and reminded him of his ministry as a disciple. How do you think Peter must have felt after he denied Jesus three times? Why do you think he went back to his old profession of fishing?

- Why do you think the disciples fished all night, but caught nothing? What do you think God might be teaching them by this?

- What did Jesus instruct the disciples to do with their fishing net and what was the result? Why do you think Peter jumped into the sea to swim to Jesus instead of waiting on the boat to come to shore?

- When the boat came ashore, what had Jesus prepared for His disciples? What do you think it would be like to have breakfast with the risen Christ?

- After breakfast, what question did Jesus ask Peter? How many times did He ask this question? How did Peter respond each time? What did Jesus remind Peter to do each time? Why do you this was repeated three times?

- In spite of his faults and failures, what is Jesus holding Peter accountable to do? In what ways is Jesus' loving spiritual accountability with Peter, *an example to follow* as we walk in accountability with one another?

- When we make big mistakes in our spiritual lives, why do we often feel like giving up? How does Peter's life prove that in spite of your sins, failures and insecurities, God can still use you to do big things?

PRAYER:

Let's pray today that God will show us clearly what He wants us to do and that we will follow Him without reservation in spite of our mistakes.

PRAYER REQUESTS:

BI-MONTHLY MISSION PROJECT NOTES:

WEEK 19

ACTS 2   [CIRCLE ONE: S P A C E]
Personal Study Notes: _____
_____
_____
_____

ACTS 3   [CIRCLE ONE: S P A C E]
Personal Study Notes: _____
_____
_____
_____

ACTS 4   [CIRCLE ONE: S P A C E]
Personal Study Notes: _____
_____
_____
_____

ACTS 5   [CIRCLE ONE: S P A C E]
Personal Study Notes: _____
_____
_____
_____

ACTS 6   [CIRCLE ONE: S P A C E]
Personal Study Notes: _____
_____
_____
_____

Read carefully one chapter of the Bible five days a week. In each chapter look for a . . .
Sin to Confess / **P**romise to Claim / **A**ttitude to Change / **C**ommand to Obey / **E**xample to Follow.

THE BEGINNING OF THE CHURCH
(ACTS 2:36-47)

WEEKLY ASSIGNMENTS:

Lead Prayer Time: _____

Tell the Story (Paraphrase): _____

Read the Text: _____

Facilitate Bible Study: _____

DISCUSSION QUESTIONS:

- Where was the first church that you ever attended? What is your most memorable experience about attending church?

- In our story, the church began in Jerusalem as three thousand believers were baptized. When Peter preached at the Feast of Pentecost, what did he say that all the house of Israel needed to know about Jesus Christ?

- What happened in the hearts of the Jews who heard Peter's message? What important question did they ask Peter and what was his response? What does it mean to "repent?" What does it mean to be "baptized" and why is baptism important? In whose name are believers to be baptized?

- What is the connection between Jesus Christ and "the forgiveness of our sins?" What special gift did Peter say that believers would receive after they are saved? Who is the "Holy Spirit" and what is His role in a believer's life?

- When did those who received Peter's message get baptized? How many of them were baptized? If you have been baptized, can you share about the experience of your baptism and what it meant to you?

- What four spiritual disciplines did these new believers immediately devote themselves to? Why are these four things important for your spiritual growth? What would have happened had they not been devoted to these things? In what ways does our D-Group help you practice these disciplines?

- What changes immediately took place in the lives of these new believers? What changed about their attitudes toward their possessions?

- What did these new believers continue to do "day by day?" How is this *an example for us to follow*? In the church today, what do you think it would take for the Lord to add to our number daily those who are being saved?

PRAYER:

Let's pray today for devotion to the disciplines required for our spiritual growth.

PRAYER REQUESTS:

BI-MONTHLY MISSION PROJECT NOTES:

WEEK 20

Weekly Bible Reading: .... Acts 7-11
Weekly Bible Study: .... Acts 8:26-40

ACTS 7   [CIRCLE ONE: S P A C E]
Personal Study Notes: _____

_____

_____

_____

ACTS 8   [CIRCLE ONE: S P A C E]
Personal Study Notes: _____

_____

_____

_____

ACTS 9   [CIRCLE ONE: S P A C E]
Personal Study Notes: _____

_____

_____

_____

ACTS 10   [CIRCLE ONE: S P A C E]
Personal Study Notes: _____

_____

_____

_____

ACTS 11   [CIRCLE ONE: S P A C E]
Personal Study Notes: _____

_____

_____

_____

Read carefully one chapter of the Bible five days a week. In each chapter look for a . . .
Sin to Confess / **P**romise to Claim / **A**ttitude to Change / **C**ommand to Obey / **E**xample to Follow.

PHILIP AND THE ETHIOPIAN EUNUCH
(ACTS 8:26-40)

WEEKLY ASSIGNMENTS:

Lead Prayer Time: _____

Tell the Story (Paraphrase): _____

Read the Text: _____

Facilitate Bible Study: _____

DISCUSSION QUESTIONS:

- Have you ever shared your faith with a complete stranger? If yes, how did it go? Why do you think you do not share the gospel more often?

- In our story, a Christian named Philip was led by God to share the Gospel with a stranger who was a high-ranking official from Ethiopia. Who directed Philip to go south to the road that goes from Jerusalem to Gaza? What are angels and in what ways do they serve God today?

- What kind of place was Philip directed to go to? Why was this a challenging assignment to obey? How did Philip respond to this assignment?

- What are we told about the man from Ethiopia? What was he doing while riding in his chariot? Who directed Philip to go over to the Ethiopian and join his chariot? How did Philip respond to the Spirit's leadership? In what ways does God's Spirit lead and direct us today?

- What is significant about the passage from Isaiah that the Ethiopian was reading? What did the Ethiopian ask Philip and what did Philip tell him about this passage? What does this tell us about Philip's knowledge of the Bible? What would have happened to the Ethiopian if Philip had not obeyed God?

- What did the Ethiopian want to do after hearing the good news about Jesus? How is the Ethiopian's baptism described? Why do you think the Lord carried Philip away right after he baptized the Ethiopian? What did he do in Azotus?

- How can you become more sensitive to the leadership of the Holy Spirit? If you were sensitive to His leadership, do you think the Spirit would lead you to witness to others more often? Why or why not?

- What do you need to do to be more prepared to witness to others? What will happen to others if you do not obey God when He leads you to witness to them? What do you intend to do about this?

PRAYER:

Let's pray today that we will become more sensitive to the leadership of the Holy Spirit and that we will have more courage in sharing our faith.

PRAYER REQUESTS:

BI-MONTHLY MISSION PROJECT NOTES:

WEEK

Weekly Bible Reading: .... Acts 12-16
Weekly Bible Study: .... Acts 12:1-17

ACTS 12 [CIRCLE ONE: S P A C E]

Personal Study Notes: _____

_____

_____

_____

ACTS 13 [CIRCLE ONE: S P A C E]

Personal Study Notes: _____

_____

_____

_____

ACTS 14 [CIRCLE ONE: S P A C E]

Personal Study Notes: _____

_____

_____

_____

ACTS 15 [CIRCLE ONE: S P A C E]

Personal Study Notes: _____

_____

_____

_____

ACTS 16 [CIRCLE ONE: S P A C E]

Personal Study Notes: _____

_____

_____

_____

Read carefully one chapter of the Bible five days a week. In each chapter look for a . . .
Sin to Confess / **P**romise to Claim / **A**ttitude to Change / **C**ommand to Obey / **E**xample to Follow.

PETER IS RESCUED BY PRAYER
(ACTS 12:1-17)

WEEKLY ASSIGNMENTS:

Lead Prayer Time: _____

Tell the Story (Paraphrase): _____

Read the Text: _____

Facilitate Bible Study: _____

DISCUSSION QUESTIONS:

* How does it make you feel when you know others are praying for you? Do you believe that prayer can change the circumstances of your life? Why or why not? Can you share a testimony about this?

* In our story, Peter was rescued from prison by prayer. Before Peter was arrested, who was the first of the twelve apostles to be martyred for his faith? Who was it that had him martyred and why do you think he did this?

* What do you think King Herod's intentions were for Peter? What season was it when Peter was arrested, and how did this work for Peter's good? Why do you think Herod ordered for Peter to be so securely guarded?

* What did the church in Jerusalem gather to do for Peter? How quickly did they gather? How is this an *example for us to follow*?

- On the night before he faced execution, why do you think Peter was able to sleep? What must the guards have been thinking about Peter? Who was it that came to help Peter? From this story and last week's story, what are we learning about the work of God's angels?

- In what miraculous ways did pray change the circumstances of Peter's life? When those at the prayer meeting heard that Peter was at the door, how did they respond? What should have been their response? What does this reveal about their faith? What does this teach us about God?

- In what ways is our faith often like the people at this prayer meeting? What do you think happened to their faith after Peter was rescued? What would have happened to Peter if the church had not prayed for him at all?

- Do you believe that God does miracles today in response to prayer? Why or why not? How does our study of this story affect your faith? How should it affect your prayer life?

PRAYER:

Let's pray earnestly today for someone who needs a miracle from God.

PRAYER REQUESTS:

BI-MONTHLY MISSION PROJECT NOTES:

WEEK

Weekly Bible Reading: . . . . Acts 17-21
Weekly Bible Study: . . . . Acts 17:1-9

ACTS 17   [CIRCLE ONE: S P A C E]
Personal Study Notes: _____

_____

_____

_____

ACTS 18   [CIRCLE ONE: S P A C E]
Personal Study Notes: _____

_____

_____

_____

ACTS 19   [CIRCLE ONE: S P A C E]
Personal Study Notes: _____

_____

_____

_____

ACTS 20   [CIRCLE ONE: S P A C E]
Personal Study Notes: _____

_____

_____

_____

ACTS 21   [CIRCLE ONE: S P A C E]
Personal Study Notes: _____

_____

_____

_____

Read carefully one chapter of the Bible five days a week. In each chapter look for a . . .
Sin to Confess / **P**romise to Claim / **A**ttitude to Change / **C**ommand to Obey / **E**xample to Follow.

TURNING THE WORLD UPSIDE DOWN
(ACTS 17:1-9)

WEEKLY ASSIGNMENTS:

Lead Prayer Time: _____

Tell the Story (Paraphrase): _____

Read the Text: _____

Facilitate Bible Study: _____

DISCUSSION QUESTIONS:

- Can you share about a time that you did something you knew would get you in trouble? Knowing the consequences, why did you do it?

- In our story, Paul and Silas were accused by the Jews in Thessalonica of turning the world upside down. Paul and Silas knew that preaching about Jesus would get them in trouble, but why do you think they did it anyway?

- On their missionary journey, what was the custom of Paul and his friends when they entered a new city like Thessalonica? What was a synagogue? How many Sabbaths did Paul go there to reason with the Jews in this city?

- How would you explain to someone that it was necessary for Christ to suffer and die? How would you explain that it was necessary for Him to rise from the dead? What did Paul mean by saying, "This Jesus whom I preach to you is the Christ?"

- Who was persuaded to believe Paul's message? What did the Jews do who were not persuaded and who were jealous of Paul? Who was Jason and why did they attack his house?

- Throughout history, why do you think unbelievers have persecuted Christians? In what ways is this happening today? How is the boldness of Paul and his friends an *example to follow* when we are persecuted for our faith?

- When the Jews came before the city authorities, what accusation did they make concerning Paul and his friends? What does this tell us about the impact that Paul and his fellow missionaries were making in the world?

- What would it take for the church in today's world to turn the world upside down for Christ? What are you doing personally to help make this happen?

PRAYER:

Let's pray today that the church would once again be filled with power and courage to turn the world upside down for Christ.

PRAYER REQUESTS:

BI-MONTHLY MISSION PROJECT NOTES:

WEEK

ACTS 22   [CIRCLE ONE: S P A C E]
Personal Study Notes: _____

_____

_____

_____

ACTS 23   [CIRCLE ONE: S P A C E]
Personal Study Notes: _____

_____

_____

_____

ACTS 24   [CIRCLE ONE: S P A C E]
Personal Study Notes: _____

_____

_____

_____

ACTS 25   [CIRCLE ONE: S P A C E]
Personal Study Notes: _____

_____

_____

_____

ACTS 26   [CIRCLE ONE: S P A C E]
Personal Study Notes: _____

_____

_____

_____

Read carefully one chapter of the Bible five days a week. In each chapter look for a . . .
Sin to Confess / **P**romise to Claim / **A**ttitude to Change / **C**ommand to Obey / **E**xample to Follow.

ALMOST PERSUADED
(ACTS 26:9-29)

WEEKLY ASSIGNMENTS:

Lead Prayer Time: _____

Tell the Story (Paraphrase): _____

Read the Text: _____

Facilitate Bible Study: _____

DISCUSSION QUESTIONS:

- What is a believer's personal testimony? What kind of things should you share in your personal testimony? Why is your testimony a powerful tool in witnessing for Christ? When is the last time you shared your testimony?

- In our story, Paul shared his personal testimony before Jewish King Agrippa while in prison in Caesarea. According to Paul, what was his life like before he came to Jesus? How did he come to know Jesus as his Savior? What was his life like after he came to Jesus?

- After Paul's conversion to Christ, what message did he declare in Damascus and in Jerusalem and throughout all Judea? Why did Paul say that the Jews seized him and tried to kill him? Who did Paul say that came to help him?

- When Governor Felix accused Paul of being "out of his mind," what was Paul's response to this accusation? What did Paul say about King Agrippa's knowledge of his testimony?

- What question did Paul ask King Agrippa? How did the king respond to Paul's question? Why is it so tragic for someone to be "almost persuaded" to become a Christian? What should be our response to someone who is "almost persuaded" to trust in Christ?

- If someone is almost persuaded to become a Christian, what will happen when this person dies? If you know someone like this, what should you pray for him or her? What things could you do for him or her?

- If you fail to share your personal testimony with others, why is this a *sin to confess*? How could you be better prepared to share your testimony? Is one person's testimony more powerful than another's? Why or why not? If you were saved as a child, why is your testimony still powerful and effective?

- Can one of you share your personal testimony with us right now?

PRAYER:

Let's pray today for more conviction and boldness in sharing our personal testimony with those who are lost.

PRAYER REQUESTS:

BI-MONTHLY MISSION PROJECT NOTES:

WEEK 24

Weekly Bible Reading: .... Acts 27 – Romans 3
Weekly Bible Study: .... Romans 1:8-17

ACTS 27   [CIRCLE ONE: S P A C E]
Personal Study Notes: _____
_____
_____
_____

ACTS 28   [CIRCLE ONE: S P A C E]
Personal Study Notes: _____
_____
_____
_____

ROMANS 1   [CIRCLE ONE: S P A C E]
Personal Study Notes: _____
_____
_____
_____

ROMANS 2   [CIRCLE ONE: S P A C E]
Personal Study Notes: _____
_____
_____
_____

ROMANS 3   [CIRCLE ONE: S P A C E]
Personal Study Notes: _____
_____
_____
_____

Read carefully one chapter of the Bible five days a week. In each chapter look for a . . .
Sin to Confess / **P**romise to Claim / **A**ttitude to Change / **C**ommand to Obey / **E**xample to Follow.

NOT ASHAMED OF THE GOSPEL
(ROMANS 1:8-17)

WEEKLY ASSIGNMENTS:

Lead Prayer Time: _____

Tell the Story (Paraphrase): _____

Read the Text: _____

Facilitate Bible Study: _____

DISCUSSION QUESTIONS:

- What is one place you have always wanted to visit, but have never been able go there? What has prevented you from going?

- In our text, Paul expressed his great desire to go to Rome, but explained that he had been prevented. Paul was thankful to God for the Roman believers because of what main thing? How often did he pray for them and what was his request?

- For what two reasons did Paul long to see the believers in Rome? What are "spiritual gifts" and how are they used to strengthen the church? What do you think your spiritual gifts are? How are you using them? In what ways are true believers "mutually encouraged" by each other's faith?

- Why did Paul say that he was "not ashamed of the gospel?" What are the basic truths of the gospel? How is the gospel the power of God for salvation to everyone who believers? In what way is this a great *promise to claim*?

- What did Paul say was revealed through the gospel? What is the "righteousness of God" and how is it different from our own righteousness? Why must everyone receive the "righteousness of God" in order to be saved?

- What did Paul mean by saying that the righteousness of God was revealed from "faith to faith?" Why must the righteous "live by faith?"

- Are you ever ashamed of the gospel? Why or why not? What would cause someone to be ashamed of the gospel? If you are not ashamed of the gospel, what must you do with the gospel? Why is this important?

- When you share the gospel with someone who is lost, is the person's salvation dependent on you or the "power of the gospel?" How does knowing this set you free to share the gospel with more confidence?

PRAYER:

Let's pray today that we will never be ashamed of the gospel, but that we will share it often with those who are lost.

PRAYER REQUESTS:

BI-MONTHLY MISSION PROJECT NOTES:

WEEK

Weekly Bible Reading: .... Romans 4-8
Weekly Bible Study: .... Romans 5:1-11

ROMANS 4   [CIRCLE ONE: S P A C E]
Personal Study Notes: _____

_____

_____

_____

ROMANS 5   [CIRCLE ONE: S P A C E]
Personal Study Notes: _____

_____

_____

_____

ROMANS 6   [CIRCLE ONE: S P A C E]
Personal Study Notes: _____

_____

_____

_____

ROMANS 7   [CIRCLE ONE: S P A C E]
Personal Study Notes: _____

_____

_____

_____

ROMANS 8   [CIRCLE ONE: S P A C E]
Personal Study Notes: _____

_____

_____

_____

Read carefully one chapter of the Bible five days a week. In each chapter look for a . . .
Sin to Confess / **P**romise to Claim / **A**ttitude to Change / **C**ommand to Obey / **E**xample to Follow.

PEACE WITH GOD
(ROMANS 5:1-11)

WEEKLY ASSIGNMENTS:

Lead Prayer Time: _____

Tell the Story (Paraphrase): _____

Read the Text: _____

Facilitate Bible Study: _____

DISCUSSION QUESTIONS:

- Is there any person or cause you would be willing to give your life for? If so, for whom or for what are you willing to make such a costly sacrifice?

- In our text, Paul taught that we could have peace with God through our Lord Jesus Christ. What did Jesus do for us so that we could have peace with God? What does it mean to be "justified by faith" and what does this have to do with having "peace with God?" How does it feel to have peace with God?

- What did Paul mean by saying that a believer has "obtained access by faith into God's grace?" In what practical ways does having access to God's grace change our lives and give us hope?

- If we have access to God's grace, why do believers still suffer harm? What things did Paul say that a believer can "know" about suffering? What purpose does suffering serve in a believer's life? How does this knowledge confront us with *an attitude to change* regarding our times of suffering?

- According to Paul, how is God's love "poured into our hearts?" When God pours His love into our hearts, how will our lives be different?

- In what truly remarkable way did God demonstrate His great love for us? In light of this, why is it impossible for us to question God's love for us?

- Having been justified by the blood of Christ, what are we certain to be saved from? Apart from the blood of Christ, what else can wash away our sin and save us from the wrath of God?

- Since we have been "reconciled to God by the death of His Son," is it wrong for us to doubt our salvation? Why or why not? Why is better to "rejoice in God" than to doubt His promise concerning our eternal salvation?

- How does it feel to know for certain that you have the assurance of eternal life with God in heaven? How does this change the way you live for God? How does this change the way you worship and serve God?

PRAYER:

Let's pray today giving God thanks for our assurance of eternal life in heaven and for the difference this makes in our lives.

PRAYER REQUESTS:

BI-MONTHLY MISSION PROJECT NOTES:

WEEK 26

Weekly Bible Reading: .... Romans 9-13
Weekly Bible Study: .... Romans 10:1-17

ROMANS 9 [CIRCLE ONE: S P A C E]
Personal Study Notes: _____
_____
_____
_____

ROMANS 10 [CIRCLE ONE: S P A C E]
Personal Study Notes: _____
_____
_____
_____

ROMANS 11 [CIRCLE ONE: S P A C E]
Personal Study Notes: _____
_____
_____
_____

ROMANS 12 [CIRCLE ONE: S P A C E]
Personal Study Notes: _____
_____
_____
_____

ROMANS 13 [CIRCLE ONE: S P A C E]
Personal Study Notes: _____
_____
_____
_____

Read carefully one chapter of the Bible five days a week. In each chapter look for a . . .
Sin to Confess / **P**romise to Claim / **A**ttitude to Change / **C**ommand to Obey / **E**xample to Follow.

FAITH COMES BY HEARING
(ROMANS 10:1-17)

WEEKLY ASSIGNMENTS:

Lead Prayer Time: _____

Tell the Story (Paraphrase): _____

Read the Text: _____

Facilitate Bible Study: _____

DISCUSSION QUESTIONS:

- Why is it often hard for us to admit when we are wrong? When is the last time you were wrong about something and who did you have to admit it to?

- In our text, Paul confessed that his fellow Jews had a zeal for God, but they were wrong about the way of salvation. According to Paul, what was his heart's desire and prayer to God for his fellow Jews? Why is it important to pray for lost people? What kind of things should we pray for them?

- Why is it hard for those who trust in their own good works to submit to the Gospel? How is it that Christ is the "end of the law for righteousness" to everyone who believers?

- In verses 9, what two things did Paul say you must do to be saved? What does it mean to confess Jesus "*as Lord*"? What does it mean to believe in "*your heart*" that God raised Him from the dead? In verse 13, what did Paul say would happen to "*everyone*" who calls on the name of the Lord?

- If a lost person never hears about Jesus, how will he or she be saved? If you never tell a lost person about Jesus, what will happen to him or her? What happens when you do tell a lost person about Jesus? Who did Paul say has beautiful feet? What do you think Paul meant by this?

- What did Paul mean by saying that "faith comes by hearing?" What must a lost person "hear" in order to be saved? Can a lost person be saved simply by observing your good works? Why or why not? How does this confront us with an *attitude to change*?

- How burdened are you for the lost to be saved? In what ways is your burden for the lost expressed? If you are not prepared or willing to share the gospel with the lost, what will you do about this?

PRAYER:

Let's pray today for a lost person that you know and pray that God will give you an opportunity to share the gospel with him or her.

PRAYER REQUESTS:

BI-MONTHLY MISSION PROJECT NOTES:

WEEK

ROMANS 14   [CIRCLE ONE: S P A C E]

Personal Study Notes: _____

_____

_____

_____

ROMANS 15   [CIRCLE ONE: S P A C E]

Personal Study Notes: _____

_____

_____

_____

ROMANS 16   [CIRCLE ONE: S P A C E]

Personal Study Notes: _____

_____

_____

_____

1 CORINTHIANS 1   [CIRCLE ONE: S P A C E]

Personal Study Notes: _____

_____

_____

_____

1 CORINTHIANS 2   [CIRCLE ONE: S P A C E]

Personal Study Notes: _____

_____

_____

_____

Read carefully one chapter of the Bible five days a week. In each chapter look for a . . .
Sin to Confess / **P**romise to Claim / **A**ttitude to Change / **C**ommand to Obey / **E**xample to Follow.

THE FOOLISHNESS OF THE CROSS
(1 CORINTHIANS 1:18-31)

WEEKLY ASSIGNMENTS:

Lead Prayer Time: _____

Tell the Story (Paraphrase): _____

Read the Text: _____

Facilitate Bible Study: _____

DISCUSSION QUESTIONS:

• Why do you think many people like wear crosses as jewelry or tattoos? How do you feel about this?

• In our text, Paul spoke about the message of the cross and how this message was viewed by the world? What is the true "message of the Cross?" Why do some people view the message of the cross as foolishness? How do those who are being saved view the message of the cross?

• What is the difference between godly wisdom and worldly wisdom? In what ways has God made foolish the wisdom of this world? What does Paul say that God will do to the wisdom of world?

• Paul said, "We preach Christ crucified" (v. 23). Why was this message of the cross a "stumbling block" to some? In what ways was this message the power and wisdom of God to others?

- What did Paul mean by saying, "The foolishness of God is wiser than men, and the weakness of God is stronger than men?" Why do you think the intellectual and affluent often resist the simple message of the gospel?

- In what ways does God use the foolish things of the world to shame the wise? How does God use the weak things of the world to shame the strong? According to Paul, why does God do this? In what ways is worldly pride and boasting a *sin to confess*?

- According to Paul (v. 31), what is the one thing that every believer should boast about? Read Galatians 6:14. How do these two verses relate and what do you learn from them?

- If you could stand before the world right now and boast of the Lord and of His cross, what things would you say?

PRAYER:

Let's pray today that we will never boast in ourselves, but only in the cross of our Lord Jesus Christ.

PRAYER REQUESTS:

BI-MONTHLY MISSION PROJECT NOTES:

WEEK 28

1 CORINTHIANS 3   [CIRCLE ONE: S P A C E]
Personal Study Notes: _____
_____
_____
_____

1 CORINTHIANS 4   [CIRCLE ONE: S P A C E]
Personal Study Notes: _____
_____
_____
_____

1 CORINTHIANS 5   [CIRCLE ONE: S P A C E]
Personal Study Notes: _____
_____
_____
_____

1 CORINTHIANS 6   [CIRCLE ONE: S P A C E]
Personal Study Notes: _____
_____
_____
_____

1 CORINTHIANS 7   [CIRCLE ONE: S P A C E]
Personal Study Notes: _____
_____
_____
_____

Read carefully one chapter of the Bible five days a week. In each chapter look for a . . .
Sin to Confess / **P**romise to Claim / **A**ttitude to Change / **C**ommand to Obey / **E**xample to Follow.

BABES IN CHRIST
(1 CORINTHIANS 3:1-17)

WEEKLY ASSIGNMENTS:

Lead Prayer Time: _____

Tell the Story (Paraphrase): _____

Read the Text: _____

Facilitate Bible Study: _____

DISCUSSION QUESTIONS:

- If you are a Christian, how long have you been committed to Christ? How much do you think you have grown in your faith during this time?

- In our text, Paul rebuked believers in the church at Corinth for their spiritual immaturity. Why do you think Paul referred to them as "babes in Christ?" What is the difference between "spiritual milk" and "solid food" and why was Paul still feeding them spiritual milk?

- In what ways were the believers at Corinth acting like carnal spiritual babies? According to Paul, what can we say is true of churches today that are full of envy, strife, and division?

- Who were Paul and Apollos and why were their names associated with division in the Corinthian church? What did Paul mean when he said, "I planted, Apollos watered, but God gave the increase?" Why is it helpful to our spiritual growth to have different types of spiritual leaders in our lives?

- Who are some of the people that God has used to invest in your life and to help you grow in your faith? Who are you investing in and helping to grow?

- What did Paul say about the judgment of a believer's works? Does the judgment of a believer's works change anything about his or her eternal salvation? Why or why not? If you are eternally saved, why should you care about the judgment of your spiritual works?

- Who is the Holy Spirit and in what ways is a believer's body a "temple of the Holy Spirit?" When did your body become the temple of the Holy Spirit?

- Since your body is the temple of the Holy Spirit, what *attitudes do you need to change* about the way you treat your body? What difference has it made in your life for the Holy Spirit of God to dwell within you?

PRAYER:

Let's pray today for God to give us a greater hunger for the solid food of God's Word and that we will grow into mature believers in Christ.

PRAYER REQUESTS:

BI-MONTHLY MISSION PROJECT NOTES:

WEEK 29

Weekly Bible Reading: .... 1 Corinthians 8-12
Weekly Bible Study: .... 1 Corinthians 9:19-27

1 CORINTHIANS 8   [CIRCLE ONE: S P A C E]
Personal Study Notes: _____

_____

_____

_____

1 CORINTHIANS 9   [CIRCLE ONE: S P A C E]
Personal Study Notes: _____

_____

_____

_____

1 CORINTHIANS 10   [CIRCLE ONE: S P A C E]
Personal Study Notes: _____

_____

_____

_____

1 CORINTHIANS 11   [CIRCLE ONE: S P A C E]
Personal Study Notes: _____

_____

_____

_____

1 CORINTHIANS 12   [CIRCLE ONE: S P A C E]
Personal Study Notes: _____

_____

_____

_____

Read carefully one chapter of the Bible five days a week. In each chapter look for a . . .
Sin to Confess / **P**romise to Claim / **A**ttitude to Change / **C**ommand to Obey / **E**xample to Follow.

BECOMING A SERVANT TO ALL
(1 CORINTHIANS 9:19-27)

WEEKLY ASSIGNMENTS:

Lead Prayer Time: _____

Tell the Story (Paraphrase): _____

Read the Text: _____

Facilitate Bible Study: _____

DISCUSSION QUESTIONS:

- Do you consider yourself a competitive person? If so, in what sports do you like to compete?

- In our text, Paul was competitive in seeking to win souls for Christ. What did Paul mean by saying that he was free from all men? Why was Paul willing to make himself a servant to all men? What did Paul mean by saying, "I have become all things to all men, that I might by all means save some?"

- What different groups of people did Paul specifically say he wanted to win to Christ? In what ways do you think Paul sacrificed to win these different groups of people to Christ? In what ways is this an *example for us to follow* today?

- How did Paul compare the Christian life to a race? What kind of crown should a Christian strive for? What role does personal discipline or self-control play in winning a race? What role does spiritual discipline play in the Christian life?

- What are some of the important spiritual disciplines necessary for Christian growth and living? What spiritual disciplines come the easiest for you? What spiritual disciplines are the most difficult for you?

- What does it mean to run the spiritual race aimlessly? Why do you think many believers today live without a sense of purpose in their spiritual lives? Does God have a purpose for every life?

- What does it mean to become spiritually disqualified? How can Christians disqualify themselves from becoming all that God wants them to be?

- As a result of this study, what personal spiritual disciplines do you need to improve on in your life? What will you do to accomplish this?

PRAYER:

Let's pray today that God will help us to practice the spiritual disciplines that He has provided for us to grow in our Christian walk.

PRAYER REQUESTS:

BI-MONTHLY MISSION PROJECT NOTES:

WEEK

1 CORINTHIANS 13   [CIRCLE ONE: S P A C E]

Personal Study Notes: _____

_____

_____

_____

1 CORINTHIANS 14   [CIRCLE ONE: S P A C E]

Personal Study Notes: _____

_____

_____

_____

1 CORINTHIANS 15   [CIRCLE ONE: S P A C E]

Personal Study Notes: _____

_____

_____

_____

1 CORINTHIANS 16   [CIRCLE ONE: S P A C E]

Personal Study Notes: _____

_____

_____

_____

2 CORINTHIANS 1   [CIRCLE ONE: S P A C E]

Personal Study Notes: _____

_____

_____

_____

Read carefully one chapter of the Bible five days a week. In each chapter look for a . . .
Sin to Confess / **P**romise to Claim / **A**ttitude to Change / **C**ommand to Obey / **E**xample to Follow.

BUT BY THE GRACE OF GOD
(1 CORINTHIANS 15:1-11)

WEEKLY ASSIGNMENTS:

Lead Prayer Time: _____

Tell the Story (Paraphrase): _____

Read the Text: _____

Facilitate Bible Study: _____

DISCUSSION QUESTIONS:

- How does the resurrection of Jesus separate Christianity from other religions? What evidence is there that Jesus really was raised?

- In our text, Paul shared about the meaning of the gospel and the resurrection of Jesus Christ. What does the word "gospel" mean? How is a person saved by the gospel? What does it mean for us to "stand" in the gospel?

- What are the three main components of the gospel that Paul preached? What emotions do you feel when you think about the fact that Christ died for your sins?

- What would it mean to the gospel if Christ had not risen from the dead? Who were all those that Paul said were eyewitnesses of the resurrected Christ? Why is this important?

- Of the group of 500 who saw Jesus alive, why is it significant that most of them were still alive at the time of Paul's writing this letter? Who was the last person to see the resurrected Christ? Why did Paul think of himself as the least of the apostles?

- What did Paul mean by saying, "By the grace of God I am what I am?" In what ways can you relate to this statement? Where would you be today apart from the grace of God? What did Paul mean by saying, "His grace toward me was not in vain?" How can you take the grace of God in vain?

- Out of gratitude for God's grace, Paul said he worked harder than them all (v. 10). How is this *an example for us to follow*? How does the grace of God work within a believer? In what ways is the grace of God is working in you today?

PRAYER:

Let's pray today that God's grace will work in us mightily and that His grace toward us will not be in vain.

PRAYER REQUESTS:

BI-MONTHLY MISSION PROJECT NOTES:

WEEK 31

Weekly Bible Reading: .... 2 Corinthians 2-6
Weekly Bible Study: .... 2 Corinthians 5:17-21

2 CORINTHIANS 2   [CIRCLE ONE: S P A C E]
*Personal Study Notes:*_____

_____

_____

_____

2 CORINTHIANS 3   [CIRCLE ONE: S P A C E]
*Personal Study Notes:*_____

_____

_____

_____

2 CORINTHIANS 4   [CIRCLE ONE: S P A C E]
*Personal Study Notes:*_____

_____

_____

_____

2 CORINTHIANS 5   [CIRCLE ONE: S P A C E]
*Personal Study Notes:*_____

_____

_____

_____

2 CORINTHIANS 6   [CIRCLE ONE: S P A C E]
*Personal Study Notes:*_____

_____

_____

_____

Read carefully one chapter of the Bible five days a week. In each chapter look for a . . .
Sin to Confess / **P**romise to Claim / **A**ttitude to Change / **C**ommand to Obey / **E**xample to Follow.

AMBASSADORS FOR CHRIST
(2 CORINTHIANS 5:17-21)

WEEKLY ASSIGNMENTS:

Lead Prayer Time: _____

Tell the Story (Paraphrase): _____

Read the Text: _____

Facilitate Bible Study: _____

DISCUSSION QUESTIONS:

- If you could start your life over again, what is one thing you would do different? What is one thing you would do the same?

- In our text, Paul said that if anyone is in Christ, he or she is a new creation. What does it mean to be "in Christ?" In what ways does a true believer become a new creation? What things pass away? What things become new?

- What does the word "reconcile" mean? Why do all people need to be reconciled with God? How does one become reconciled with God? What is the "ministry of reconciliation" that God has entrusted to us? In what ways are we to fulfill this ministry? How important is this ministry?

- What is the "message of reconciliation?" What does it mean that God does not "count" or "impute" our trespasses against us? How does this wonderful *promise to claim* help us overcome feelings of guilt?

- What is an ambassador and in what ways are we "ambassadors for Christ" on earth? What is our main assignment as His ambassadors? As an ambassador for Christ, do you consider yourself a good one or bad one and why?

- Who is "Him who knew no sin?" When did "Him who knew no sin become sin for us?" Since Jesus became sin for us, what did He give to us in exchange?

- How does it make you feel to possess as an eternal treasure the "imputed" righteousness of God? Because of this truth, how are you growing in "personal" righteousness?

PRAYER:

Let's pray today that God will help us to be committed and courageous ambassadors for Christ.

PRAYER REQUESTS:

BI-MONTHLY MISSION PROJECT NOTES:

WEEK 32

Weekly Bible Reading: .... 2 Corinthians 7-11
Weekly Bible Study: .... 2 Corinthians 9:6-15

2 CORINTHIANS 7 [CIRCLE ONE: S P A C E]

*Personal Study Notes:*_____

_____

_____

_____

2 CORINTHIANS 8 [CIRCLE ONE: S P A C E]

*Personal Study Notes:*_____

_____

_____

_____

2 CORINTHIANS 9 [CIRCLE ONE: S P A C E]

*Personal Study Notes:*_____

_____

_____

_____

2 CORINTHIANS 10 [CIRCLE ONE: S P A C E]

*Personal Study Notes:*_____

_____

_____

_____

2 CORINTHIANS 11 [CIRCLE ONE: S P A C E]

*Personal Study Notes:*_____

_____

_____

_____

Read carefully one chapter of the Bible five days a week. In each chapter look for a . . .
Sin to Confess / **P**romise to Claim / **A**ttitude to Change / **C**ommand to Obey / **E**xample to Follow.

CHEERFUL GIVING
(2 CORINTHIANS 9:6-15)

WEEKLY ASSIGNMENTS:

Lead Prayer Time: _____

Tell the Story (Paraphrase): _____

Read the Text: _____

Facilitate Bible Study: _____

DISCUSSION QUESTIONS:

- Why is it often a greater blessing to give a gift than to receive one? When you give a gift, who do you enjoy giving to the most and why?

- In our text, Paul spoke of the benefits and blessings of being a cheerful giver. In the context of giving, what did Paul mean by saying, "Whoever sows sparingly will also reap sparingly and whoever sows bountifully will also reap bountifully" (v. 6)?

- In our giving to God or others, what does it mean to give "reluctantly" or "under compulsion?" What does it mean to give to God "cheerfully?" Why do you think God loves a cheerful giver?

- According to Paul (v. 8), what is God "able" to do when we give bountifully and cheerfully? How does this *promise to claim* affect your thoughts and attitude about giving?

- According to Paul (v. 11), what is the purpose for which God brings financial increase into our lives? Do you think the majority of people today understand this truth? Why or why not?

- In what ways does generous giving provide for the ministry of the church and produce thanksgiving to God? Do you consider yourself a generous giver? Why or why not? How do you feel about giving to your church? How do you feel about giving to those in need?

- What do you think is God's "inexpressible or indescribable gift" for which Paul expresses thanks (v. 15)? When you think about God's inexpressible gift to you, how does it make you feel about your giving to Him?

PRAYER:

Let's pray today that we will be cheerful givers and that others will be blessed by our generosity.

PRAYER REQUESTS:

BI-MONTHLY MISSION PROJECT NOTES:

WEEK

Weekly Bible Reading: .... 2 Corinthians 12 – Galatians 3
Weekly Bible Study: .... 2 Corinthians 12:2-10

2 CORINTHIANS 12   [CIRCLE ONE: S P A C E]
*Personal Study Notes:*_____
_____
_____
_____

2 CORINTHIANS 13   [CIRCLE ONE: S P A C E]
*Personal Study Notes:*_____
_____
_____
_____

GALATIANS 1   [CIRCLE ONE: S P A C E]
*Personal Study Notes:*_____
_____
_____
_____

GALATIANS 2   [CIRCLE ONE: S P A C E]
*Personal Study Notes:*_____
_____
_____
_____

GALATIANS 3   [CIRCLE ONE: S P A C E]
*Personal Study Notes:*_____
_____
_____
_____

Read carefully one chapter of the Bible five days a week. In each chapter look for a . . .
Sin to Confess / **P**romise to Claim / **A**ttitude to Change / **C**ommand to Obey / **E**xample to Follow.

A THORN IN THE FLESH
(2 CORINTHIANS 12:2-10)

WEEKLY ASSIGNMENTS:

Lead Prayer Time: _____

Tell the Story (Paraphrase): _____

Read the Text: _____

Facilitate Bible Study: _____

DISCUSSION QUESTIONS:

- When people today refer to something or someone as a "thorn in the flesh," what do they mean by this? Why are thorns so painful and irritating?

- In our text, Paul shared a personal testimony about his own thorn in the flesh. At the beginning of his testimony, why do you think Paul referred to himself in third person? How many years does Paul travel back in his memories and what spectacular vision did he recall?

- What is the "third heaven" that Paul refers to (v. 2)? When Paul was "caught up" into the third heaven or paradise, what did he hear? If God gave Paul an exclusive and extraordinary glimpse of heaven, why could this have become a cause for spiritual pride and boasting?

- What did God allow in Paul's life in order to keep him from boasting? Though we cannot know for sure, what do you think Paul's "thorn in the flesh" might have been? God allowed the thorn, but who caused it?

- What was Paul's initial response to his thorn in the flesh? How many times did Paul pray for God to remove the thorn? What was God's answer to Paul's prayers? God would not take away the thorn, but what two things did He promise instead?

- How did Paul respond to God's answer to his prayers and in what ways does he provide an example to follow in dealing with thorns in our own lives?

- When we are made weak by trials, who is strong for us? Can someone give a testimony of a time when God was strong for you in a time of weakness?

- What thorns are you dealing with today? Would you rather have God remove the thorn or give you His strength and grace and why?

PRAYER:

Let's pray today that we will learn to accept the pain of fleshly thorns in exchange for God's power and grace in our lives.

PRAYER REQUESTS:

BI-MONTHLY MISSION PROJECT NOTES:

WEEK 34

Weekly Bible Reading: .... Galatians 4-Ephesians 2
Weekly Bible Study: ....Galatians 5:16-26

GALATIANS 4 [CIRCLE ONE: S P A C E]

*Personal Study Notes:*_____
_____
_____
_____

GALATIANS 5 [CIRCLE ONE: S P A C E]

*Personal Study Notes:*_____
_____
_____
_____

GALATIANS 6 [CIRCLE ONE: S P A C E]

*Personal Study Notes:*_____
_____
_____
_____

EPHESIANS 1 [CIRCLE ONE: S P A C E]

*Personal Study Notes:*_____
_____
_____
_____

EPHESIANS 2 [CIRCLE ONE: S P A C E]

*Personal Study Notes:*_____
_____
_____
_____

Read carefully one chapter of the Bible five days a week. In each chapter look for a . . .
Sin to Confess / **P**romise to Claim / **A**ttitude to Change / **C**ommand to Obey / **E**xample to Follow.

THE FRUIT OF THE SPIRIT
(GALATIANS 5:16-26)

WEEKLY ASSIGNMENTS:

Lead Prayer Time: _____

Tell the Story (Paraphrase): _____

Read the Text: _____

Facilitate Bible Study: _____

DISCUSSION QUESTIONS:

- Who is the Holy Spirit? What is your relationship with the Holy Spirit and when did this relationship begin?

- In our text, Paul commands us to walk by the Spirit and tells us about the fruit of the Spirit. As a *command to obey*, what does it mean to "walk by the Spirit" (v. 16)? What are some things that can help us obey this command?

- What is "the flesh?" In what ways are the Spirit and the flesh opposed to one another? How does the Holy Spirit assist us in our struggle against the desires of the flesh?

- What did Paul mean by saying, "If you are led by the Spirit, you are not under the law" (v. 18)? What is the relationship between the law and the Spirit in a believer's life?

- What are the "works of the flesh" (v. 19-21)? What "works of the flesh" do you struggle with most? Who did Paul say would not inherit the kingdom of God (v. 21b)? What do you think he meant by this?

- What is the "fruit of the Spirit?" How does this "fruit" grow in a believer's life? Since becoming a believer, what "fruit of the Spirit" have you seen growing in your life? In what particular fruit of the Spirit do you need to see more growth?

- Paul said, "Those who belong to Christ Jesus have crucified the flesh with its passions and desires" (v. 24)? What did he mean by this?

- How does the Spirit help us to grow in Christ-likeness? In what ways have your grown in Christ-likeness and where do you still need the most growth?

PRAYER:

Let's pray today for one another that we will walk by the Spirit and continue to grow the fruit of the Spirit.

PRAYER REQUESTS:

BI-MONTHLY MISSION PROJECT NOTES:

WEEK 35

Weekly Bible Reading: .... Ephesians 3 – Philippians 1
Weekly Bible Study: .... Ephesians 5:21-33

EPHESIANS 3   [CIRCLE ONE: S P A C E]
Personal Study Notes: _____
_____
_____
_____

EPHESIANS 4   [CIRCLE ONE: S P A C E]
Personal Study Notes: _____
_____
_____
_____

EPHESIANS 5   [CIRCLE ONE: S P A C E]
Personal Study Notes: _____
_____
_____
_____

EPHESIANS 6   [CIRCLE ONE: S P A C E]
Personal Study Notes: _____
_____
_____
_____

PHILIPPIANS 1   [CIRCLE ONE: S P A C E]
Personal Study Notes: _____
_____
_____
_____

Read carefully one chapter of the Bible five days a week. In each chapter look for a . . .
Sin to Confess / **P**romise to Claim / **A**ttitude to Change / **C**ommand to Obey / **E**xample to Follow.

PRINCIPLES FOR MARRIAGE AND DATING
(EPHESIANS 5:21-33)

WEEKLY ASSIGNMENTS:

Lead Prayer Time: _____

Tell the Story (Paraphrase): _____

Read the Text: _____

Facilitate Bible Study: _____

DISCUSSION QUESTIONS:

- Whether you are just dating, engaged, or married, why is it important to understand and apply God's principles for marriage in your relationship? Do you think these principles are timeless or outdated? Why do you think this?

- In our text, Paul instructs husbands and wives on God's principles for a Christian marriage. Why is it important for a Christian to date and to marry another Christian? Read 2 Cor. 6:14-15. What do these verses say about dating or marrying an unbeliever?

- In all Christian relationships, why is it important to "submit to one another" (v. 21)? In the marriage relationship, what specific instructions does God give to Christian wives (v. 22-24)? What do you think biblical submission means and why is it important in the marriage relationship?

- In what way is a husband to be "the head of the wife" (v. 23)? Why do you think many today often view the biblical principle of headship and submission in marriage negatively? What can we learn about this principle from Christ and His church that can help us view it more positively?

- In the marriage relationship, what specific instructions does God give to Christian husbands (v. 25-29)? The root Greek word used here for "love" is "agape," meaning sacrificial love. Following the example of Christ's love for the church, in what sacrificial ways is a Christian husband to love his wife?

- In dating or marriage, how does the reciprocal sharing of love and respect between a man and woman work to build a great relationship? What occurs when one or the other breaks down?

- In your marriage or dating relationship, how are you doing in developing and fulfilling your God-given role? What *attitude do you need to change*? What is one thing you need to ask God to help you do better?

PRAYER:

Let's pray today for God to help us have healthy marriages and dating relationships through the biblical principles of love and respect.

PRAYER REQUESTS:

BI-MONTHLY MISSION PROJECT NOTES:

WEEK 36

Weekly Bible Reading: .... Philippians 2 – Colossians 2
Weekly Bible Study: .... Philippians 2:3-13

PHILIPPIANS 2   [CIRCLE ONE: S P A C E]
*Personal Study Notes:*_____
_____
_____
_____

PHILIPPIANS 3   [CIRCLE ONE: S P A C E]
*Personal Study Notes:*_____
_____
_____
_____

PHILIPPIANS 4   [CIRCLE ONE: S P A C E]
*Personal Study Notes:*_____
_____
_____
_____

COLOSSIANS 1   [CIRCLE ONE: S P A C E]
*Personal Study Notes:*_____
_____
_____
_____

COLOSSIANS 2   [CIRCLE ONE: S P A C E]
*Personal Study Notes:*_____
_____
_____
_____

Read carefully one chapter of the Bible five days a week. In each chapter look for a . . .
Sin to Confess / **P**romise to Claim / **A**ttitude to Change / **C**ommand to Obey / **E**xample to Follow.

THE HUMILITY OF CHRIST
(PHILIPPIANS 2:3-13)

WEEKLY ASSIGNMENTS:

Lead Prayer Time: _____

Tell the Story (Paraphrase): _____

Read the Text: _____

Facilitate Bible Study: _____

DISCUSSION QUESTIONS:

- What do you think when you meet a truly humble and selfless person? What do you think when you meet a conceited and self-centered person?

- In our text, Paul exhorted believers to follow Christ's example of genuine humility and selflessness. In what practical ways we can consider others more important than ourselves? How can we look out for the interests of others and not just our own?

- What did Paul mean by exhorting believers to have the same mind as Christ Jesus regarding selfish ambition and conceit (v. 5-8)? Who was Jesus before He was born? What did Jesus become after He was born? In what ways did Jesus "empty" Himself? Why did He do this?

- What limits did Jesus place on His obedience to the Father (v. 8)? As a possible *sin to confess*, are there any areas of your life where you are practicing a limited obedience to God? If so, in what area? What are you going to do about this?

- Because Jesus humbled Himself, what did God the Father do for Him (v. 9-11)? When we practice humble obedience to God, what do you think God will do for us? Read James 4:10. How is this *a promise to claim*?

- What did Paul say that every single person would eventually do at the name of Jesus (v. 10-11)? Though every knee will bow to Jesus and every tongue confess Him as Lord, why will it be too late for many to be saved?

- What did Paul mean by saying, "work out your own salvation with fear and trembling?" Since professing Christ as your Savior, what evidences of personal salvation have you and others witnessed in your life?

PRAYER:

Let's pray today for God to give us the mind of Christ with a humble and obedient heart toward God.

PRAYER REQUESTS:

BI-MONTHLY MISSION PROJECT NOTES:

WEEK 37

Weekly Bible Reading: .... Colossians 3 – 1 Thessalonians 3
Weekly Bible Study: .... 1 Thessalonians 1:1-10

COLOSSIANS 3
[CIRCLE ONE: S P A C E]

Personal Study Notes: _____

_____

_____

_____

COLOSSIANS 4
[CIRCLE ONE: S P A C E]

Personal Study Notes: _____

_____

_____

_____

1 THESSALONIANS 1
[CIRCLE ONE: S P A C E]

Personal Study Notes: _____

_____

_____

_____

1 THESSALONIANS 2
[CIRCLE ONE: S P A C E]

Personal Study Notes: _____

_____

_____

_____

1 THESSALONIANS 3
[CIRCLE ONE: S P A C E]

Personal Study Notes: _____

_____

_____

_____

Read carefully one chapter of the Bible five days a week. In each chapter look for a . . .
Sin to Confess / **P**romise to Claim / **A**ttitude to Change / **C**ommand to Obey / **E**xample to Follow.

AN EXAMPLE FOR ALL BELIEVERS
(1 THESSALONIANS 1:1-10)

WEEKLY ASSIGNMENTS:

Lead Prayer Time: _____

Tell the Story (Paraphrase): _____

Read the Text: _____

Facilitate Bible Study: _____

DISCUSSION QUESTIONS:

- What things come to your mind when you think of a great church? What image of the church do many have today?

- In our text, Paul was thankful for the church of the Thessalonians and continually prayed for the church. Why is it important to pray for your church? What kind of things should you pray for your church?

- For what three specific things did Paul give thanks as he remembered the church of the Thessalonians (v. 2-3)? Because of your faith, love, and hope in God, what kind of good works and spiritual labor are you doing for the Lord at this time?

- How did Paul know the Thessalonian believers were "chosen" by God (v. 4-5)? What is the "gospel" and in what ways does it confront people with power and conviction? Read Romans 1:16. How powerful is the gospel?

- In what ways did the church of the Thessalonians become an example to all believers (v. 8-10)? From this church, the Word of God "sounded forth everywhere" (v. 8). How is this a great *example for us to follow*? In what ways are you helping to "sound forth" the gospel?

- What powerful testimony were others hearing about the Thessalonian believers (v. 9)? To be effect servants of "the true and living God," why is it necessary for us to turn away from worldly idols? What kind of idols do people serve today? Are you serving God or worldly idols?

- Why should we believe in the return of Jesus? What does it mean to "wait" for His return (v. 10)? Are you ready for His return? Why or why not?

- For a true believer, what did Paul say that Jesus would deliver us from? What did Jesus do for you so that He could save you from the "wrath to come?" In what ways does this motivate you to serve Him and share Him with other?

PRAYER:

Let's pray today that we will turn away from all worldly idols to serve Christ and share Him with others.

PRAYER REQUESTS:

BI-MONTHLY MISSION PROJECT NOTES:

WEEK 38

Weekly Bible Reading: . . . . .1 Thessalonians. 4 – 2 Thessalonians 3
Weekly Bible Study: . . . . 2 Thessalonians 2:1-12

1 THESSALONIANS 4 [CIRCLE ONE: S P A C E]

Personal Study Notes: _____

_____

_____

_____

1 THESSALONIANS 5 [CIRCLE ONE: S P A C E]

Personal Study Notes: _____

_____

_____

_____

2 THESSALONIANS 1 [CIRCLE ONE: S P A C E]

Personal Study Notes: _____

_____

_____

_____

2 THESSALONIANS 2 [CIRCLE ONE: S P A C E]

Personal Study Notes: _____

_____

_____

_____

2 THESSALONIANS 3 [CIRCLE ONE: S P A C E]

Personal Study Notes: _____

_____

_____

_____

Read carefully one chapter of the Bible five days a week. In each chapter look for a . . .
Sin to Confess / **P**romise to Claim / **A**ttitude to Change / **C**ommand to Obey / **E**xample to Follow.

THE MAN OF LAWLESSNESS
(2 THESSALONIANS 2:1-12)

WEEKLY ASSIGNMENTS:

Lead Prayer Time: _____

Tell the Story (Paraphrase): _____

Read the Text: _____

Facilitate Bible Study: _____

DISCUSSION QUESTIONS:

- Do you think we are living in the last days before the return of Christ? Why or why not? How can we know if we are in the last days?

- In our text, Paul answered questions and concerns the Thessalonians had about the return of Christ. As believers, do we need to be concerned about missing the return of Christ? Why or why not?

- What two things did Paul say must happen before Christ's return (v. 3)? What does Paul mean when he refers to "the falling away" or "the rebellion?" Do you think this falling away has already started? Why or why not?

- What characteristics of the Antichrist did Paul describe as "the man of lawlessness" (v. 3b-4)? Who will the Antichrist proclaim himself to be?

- Paul spoke of a force that "is restraining" the Antichrist for now (v. 6-7). Who or what do you think this force is? When do you think this force will be taken "out of the way?" What happens when the restraining force is taken away?

- What fate awaits the Antichrist at the return of Christ (v. 8)? Whose power is associated with this man of lawlessness and in what ways (v. 9)?

- Who will fall under the "wicked deception" of the Antichrist (v. 10a)? What two important things did "those who are perishing" refuse to do (v. 10b)?

- What does it mean to "love the truth?" If you refuse to love truth, why are you likely "to believe what is false?" What will happen to "all" who refuse to believe the truth but have pleasure in unrighteousness (v. 12)? How does your life show your love the truth? Is there *any sin to confess* in this area?

- What must you do to be ready for the return of Christ? If He returned today, what would be your greatest regret? What would be your greatest delight?

PRAYER:

Let's pray today that our love for truth and for Christ will grow more each day as we draw nearer to His return.

PRAYER REQUESTS:

BI-MONTHLY MISSION PROJECT NOTES:

WEEK 39

1 TIMOTHY 1   [CIRCLE ONE: S P A C E]

Personal Study Notes: _____

_____

_____

_____

1 TIMOTHY 2   [CIRCLE ONE: S P A C E]

Personal Study Notes: _____

_____

_____

_____

1 TIMOTHY 3   [CIRCLE ONE: S P A C E]

Personal Study Notes: _____

_____

_____

_____

1 TIMOTHY 4   [CIRCLE ONE: S P A C E]

Personal Study Notes: _____

_____

_____

_____

1 TIMOTHY 5   [CIRCLE ONE: S P A C E]

Personal Study Notes: _____

_____

_____

_____

Read carefully one chapter of the Bible five days a week. In each chapter look for a . . .
Sin to Confess / **P**romise to Claim / **A**ttitude to Change / **C**ommand to Obey / **E**xample to Follow.

PRAYING FOR ALL PEOPLE
(1 TIMOTHY 2:1-7)

WEEKLY ASSIGNMENTS:

Lead Prayer Time: _____

Tell the Story (Paraphrase): _____

Read the Text: _____

Facilitate Bible Study: _____

DISCUSSION QUESTIONS:

- Why is it important for us to pray? Do you believe that prayer changes things? Why or why not? Can you share a story about an answered prayer?

- In our text, Paul urged believers to pray for all people, especially those in places of authority. What did Paul imply by saying, "First of all" (v. 1)?

- What four different words for prayer did Paul use (v. 1)? How might these words suggest different ways that we should pray? Why should we praise and worship God when we pray? Why should we confess our sins? Why should we express words of thanks? Why should we pray for others?

- In addition to praying for "all people," whom specifically did Paul say we should pray for (v. 2)? Why did he say we should pray for those in "high positions" of authority? Should we pray for our leaders and other authorities even when we may not agree with them? Why or why not?

- Why do you think prayer is "pleasing in the sight of God our Savior" (v. 3)? How does it make you feel that God is pleased when you talk with Him?

- Speaking of "God our Savior," what did Paul say that God desires for "all people" to do (v. 4)? Knowing this, why is it important for us to pray for those who are lost? What kind of things should we pray for those who are lost?

- According to Paul, what did "Christ Jesus" do so that we could be reconciled with God (v. 5-6)? What does it mean that Jesus give himself as a "ransom for all?" Is Christ the only way to be reconciled with God? Why or why not?

- Concerning the testimony of Christ, what did Paul say he was "appointed" to do (v. 7)? Why is it important for all of us to share our testimony about Christ? Do you regularly share your testimony about Christ? Why or why not?

PRAYER:

Let's pray today for someone in authority and for someone who is lost.

PRAYER REQUESTS:

BI-MONTHLY MISSION PROJECT NOTES:

WEEK 40

Weekly Bible Reading: ....1 Timothy 6 – 2 Timothy 4
Weekly Bible Study: ....2 Timothy 2:1-7

1 TIMOTHY 6   [CIRCLE ONE: S P A C E]

Personal Study Notes: _____

_____

_____

_____

2 TIMOTHY 1   [CIRCLE ONE: S P A C E]

Personal Study Notes: _____

_____

_____

_____

2 TIMOTHY 2   [CIRCLE ONE: S P A C E]

Personal Study Notes: _____

_____

_____

_____

2 TIMOTHY 3   [CIRCLE ONE: S P A C E]

Personal Study Notes: _____

_____

_____

_____

2 TIMOTHY 4   [CIRCLE ONE: S P A C E]

Personal Study Notes: _____

_____

_____

_____

Read carefully one chapter of the Bible five days a week. In each chapter look for a . . .
Sin to Confess / **P**romise to Claim / **A**ttitude to Change / **C**ommand to Obey / **E**xample to Follow.

WEEK 40   **157**

AUTHENTIC DISCIPLESHIP
(2 TIMOTHY 2:1-7)

WEEKLY ASSIGNMENTS:

Lead Prayer Time: _____

Tell the Story (Paraphrase): _____

Read the Text: _____

Facilitate Bible Study: _____

DISCUSSION QUESTIONS:

- What does the word "disciple" mean? What does the process of discipleship involve? In the Christian life, why is authentic discipleship vitally important?

- In our text, Paul teaches his young disciple Timothy about discipleship. Why do you think Paul referred to Timothy as "my child" (v. 1a)? What was Timothy instructed to be "strengthened by" and for what reason (v. 1b)?

- What specific command did Paul give Timothy (v. 2)? Is this a *command for us to obey* today? Why or why not? In what ways are you obeying this command? What happens when we fail to obey this command?

- What four different generations of discipleship are cited in verse 2? Why is it necessary for authentic discipleship to continually reproduce and multiply? If it fails to multiply, is it authentic discipleship? Why or why not?

- According to Paul, in what ways is a disciple-maker like a "good soldier" (v. 3-4)? To be an effective disciple-maker, why is it essential not to get entangled in "civilian pursuits" (v. 4)? What civilian pursuits threaten your discipleship?

- According to Paul, in what ways is a disciple-maker like a disciplined "athlete" (v. 5)? What spiritual disciplines are required of disciple-makers?

- According to Paul, in what ways is a disciple-maker like a "hard-working farmer" (v. 6)? If the greatest rewards of farming are seeing crops grow and reproduce; likewise, what are the greatest rewards of disciple-making? As a disciple, when will you be ready to reproduce and to begin leading others?

- As we "think over" Paul's words (v. 7), is authentic discipleship a program or a lifestyle? Why must we train and equip all believers for a lifestyle of making and multiplying disciples? How is living the D-Life equipping you for this?

PRAYER:

Let's pray today that each of us will be equipped for a lifestyle of discipleship.

PRAYER REQUESTS:

BI-MONTHLY MISSION PROJECT NOTES:

WEEK 41

Weekly Bible Reading: ....Titus 1 – Hebrews 1
Weekly Bible Study: ....Titus 2:1-8

TITUS 1 [CIRCLE ONE: S P A C E]
Personal Study Notes: _____
_____
_____
_____

TITUS 2 [CIRCLE ONE: S P A C E]
Personal Study Notes: _____
_____
_____
_____

TITUS 3 [CIRCLE ONE: S P A C E]
Personal Study Notes: _____
_____
_____
_____

PHILEMON 1 [CIRCLE ONE: S P A C E]
Personal Study Notes: _____
_____
_____
_____

HEBREWS 1 [CIRCLE ONE: S P A C E]
Personal Study Notes: _____
_____
_____
_____

Read carefully one chapter of the Bible five days a week. In each chapter look for a . . .
Sin to Confess / **P**romise to Claim / **A**ttitude to Change / **C**ommand to Obey / **E**xample to Follow.

DISCIPLING THE NEXT GENERATION
(TITUS 2:1-8)

WEEKLY ASSIGNMENTS:

Lead Prayer Time: _____

Tell the Story (Paraphrase): _____

Read the Text: _____

Facilitate Bible Study: _____

DISCUSSION QUESTIONS:

- Who is someone that invested in your life when you were younger? What kind of things did you learn from him or her? How do you feel about this person today?

- In our text, Paul specifically instructed mature believers to train younger believers. Why is this still an important *command to obey*?

- What kind of things can a younger believer learn from an older believer? What kind of things can an older believer learn from investing in a younger believer?

- What specific qualities does Paul say are proper for men who are mature in the faith (v. 2)? What qualities does he say are proper for spiritually mature women (v. 3)? What does it mean to be sound in faith? What does it mean to be reverent in behavior?

- What did Paul say that younger women should be taught (v. 4-5)? What did Paul say that younger men should be taught (v. 6-8)?

- Is the church today doing a good job of discipling the next generation? How might the world be a different place if we were more committed to this?

- Paul instructed us in all respects to be "a model of good works" (v. 7). In what ways is your life a model of good works? In what specific areas of your life do you need to continue to grow in this?

- Knowing that God has sent people who have made great investments in your life, why should you feel responsible to invest in others?

- Realizing the importance of multi-generational discipleship, in what ways are you investing in the next generation? How is D-Life helping you with this?

PRAYER:

Let's pray today that each of us will be a model of good works and that we will continue to live an intentional lifestyle of discipleship.

PRAYER REQUESTS:

BI-MONTHLY MISSION PROJECT NOTES:

WEEK 42

Weekly Bible Reading: . . . . Hebrews 2-6
Weekly Bible Study: . . . . Hebrews 4:12-16

HEBREWS 2   [CIRCLE ONE: S P A C E]

Personal Study Notes: _____

_____

_____

_____

HEBREWS 3   [CIRCLE ONE: S P A C E]

Personal Study Notes: _____

_____

_____

_____

HEBREWS 4   [CIRCLE ONE: S P A C E]

Personal Study Notes: _____

_____

_____

_____

HEBREWS 5   [CIRCLE ONE: S P A C E]

Personal Study Notes: _____

_____

_____

_____

HEBREWS 6   [CIRCLE ONE: S P A C E]

Personal Study Notes: _____

_____

_____

_____

Read carefully one chapter of the Bible five days a week. In each chapter look for a . . .
Sin to Confess / **P**romise to Claim / **A**ttitude to Change / **C**ommand to Obey / **E**xample to Follow.

THE LIVING WORD
(HEBREWS 4:12-16)

WEEKLY ASSIGNMENTS:

Lead Prayer Time: _____

Tell the Story (Paraphrase): _____

Read the Text: _____

Facilitate Bible Study: _____

DISCUSSION QUESTIONS:

- Other than the Bible, what is the best book you have ever read? What makes the Bible more powerful than all other books?

- In our text, the Word of God is described as living and active. What do you think this means? As you read the Bible, what makes the Word of God come alive in your heart? How does this motivate you to be consistent in your daily Bible reading?

- Why do you think the Word of God is described as sharper than any "two-edged sword" (v. 12)? What do you think are the two different edges of the "sword" of Scripture? Can you give a recent example of how a certain verse or passage from the Bible has personally "pierced" your heart?

- Is the Word of God completely sufficient to impart spiritual growth and change in the life of a believer?

Why or why not? According to Hebrews, to Whom are we accountable for living by everything written in the Word of God (v. 13)? Why is it impossible to hide anything from God?

- As believers, Who is our "great high priest" (v. 14)? When did He pass "through the heavens" and what did He come to do for us? What is significant about "our confession" in Him? Why must we "hold fast" to our confession of faith in Christ? In what ways are we tempted to deny Him?

- As our great high priest, in what ways is Jesus able to sympathize with all our weaknesses and temptations (v. 15)? How does this make you feel?

- What is the "throne of grace" and what are we encouraged to do regarding this throne (v. 16)? Why can we draw near to the throne of grace "with confidence?" How do we "draw near" the throne of grace? As a *promise to claim*, what will we receive when we draw near the throne of grace?

- Can you share a testimony of a time when you drew near the throne of grace and received help from the Lord? In what ways did you find His grace and help? In what ways can we be agents of God's grace and help to others?

PRAYER:

Let's pray today for someone we know who is going through a time of need.

PRAYER REQUESTS:

BI-MONTHLY MISSION PROJECT NOTES:

WEEK 43

Weekly Bible Reading: .... Hebrews 7-11
Weekly Bible Study: .... Hebrews 11:1-12

HEBREWS 7   [CIRCLE ONE: S P A C E]

Personal Study Notes: _____

_____

_____

_____

HEBREWS 8   [CIRCLE ONE: S P A C E]

Personal Study Notes: _____

_____

_____

_____

HEBREWS 9   [CIRCLE ONE: S P A C E]

Personal Study Notes: _____

_____

_____

_____

HEBREWS 10   [CIRCLE ONE: S P A C E]

Personal Study Notes: _____

_____

_____

_____

HEBREWS 11   [CIRCLE ONE: S P A C E]

Personal Study Notes: _____

_____

_____

_____

Read carefully one chapter of the Bible five days a week. In each chapter look for a . . .
Sin to Confess / **P**romise to Claim / **A**ttitude to Change / **C**ommand to Obey / **E**xample to Follow.

HEROES OF FAITH
(HEBREWS 11:1-12)

WEEKLY ASSIGNMENTS:

Lead Prayer Time: _____

Tell the Story (Paraphrase): _____

Read the Text: _____

Facilitate Bible Study: _____

DISCUSSION QUESTIONS:

- Who is your favorite super hero? What special traits of this super hero cause you to admire him or her the most?

- In our text, we are told about some real heroes of faith. What definition of faith is given at the beginning of this chapter (v. 1)? What did "people of old" receive by their faith (v. 2) and why is this a great thing to obtain?

- What do we understand by faith about the creation of the universe (v. 3)? How is this in opposition to many modern theories of creation?

- Why was Abel's offering more acceptable to God than Cain's (v. 4)? What can we learn from Abel about giving by faith? What happened to Enoch because of his faith (v. 5)? What can we learn from Enoch about walking by faith?

- Why do you think it is "impossible to please God" without faith (v. 6)? What kind of faith does God reward? How is "seeking God" related to our faith?

- What did Noah do because of his faith (v. 7)? Why would this have been difficult to do? In Noah's situation, what do you think you would do? In what way did Noah become "an heir of the righteousness that comes by faith?"

- What did Abraham do because of his faith (v. 8)? Why would this have been difficult to do? Can you tell of a time when God called you to do something without giving you all the answers? How did you respond to this situation?

- Who was Sarah and in what ways did she share a similar faith to that of Abraham's (v. 9-11)? In dating or marriage, why is it important for us to share a "like-minded" faith with one we are in a relationship with? What incredible blessings did Abraham and Sarah receive because of their like-minded faith?

- In what ways is the faith Abel, Enoch, Noah, Abraham, and Sarah an *example for us to follow*? Of these five individuals, whose test of faith can you identify with the most and why? In what ways is God testing your faith today?

PRAYER:

Let's pray for each other today that God will help us to walk by faith and not by sight.

PRAYER REQUESTS:

BI-MONTHLY MISSION PROJECT NOTES:

WEEK

Weekly Bible Reading: ....Hebrews 12 – James 3
Weekly Bible Study: ....James 2:14-26

HEBREWS 12   [CIRCLE ONE: S P A C E]
Personal Study Notes: _____

_____

_____

_____

HEBREWS 13   [CIRCLE ONE: S P A C E]
Personal Study Notes: _____

_____

_____

_____

JAMES 1   [CIRCLE ONE: S P A C E]
Personal Study Notes: _____

_____

_____

_____

JAMES 2   [CIRCLE ONE: S P A C E]
Personal Study Notes: _____

_____

_____

_____

JAMES 3   [CIRCLE ONE: S P A C E]
Personal Study Notes: _____

_____

_____

_____

Read carefully one chapter of the Bible five days a week. In each chapter look for a . . .
Sin to Confess / **P**romise to Claim / **A**ttitude to Change / **C**ommand to Obey / **E**xample to Follow.

FAITH WITHOUT WORKS
(JAMES 2:14-26)

WEEKLY ASSIGNMENTS:

Lead Prayer Time: _____

Tell the Story (Paraphrase): _____

Read the Text: _____

Facilitate Bible Study: _____

DISCUSSION QUESTIONS:

- How does it make you feel when someone says one thing, but does another? Why do we doubt the sincerity of those whose walk and talk fail to match?

- In our text, James explained the relationship between faith and works. What question does James confront us with at the beginning of this text (v. 14)? Why is this an important question to consider?

- What real life illustration does James give to show that saying one thing and doing another is irrational and conflicting (v. 15-16)? What does James mean by saying, "So also faith by itself, if it does not have works, is dead (v. 17)?

- What evidence did James give to show that his own faith in Christ was real (v. 18)? What kind of works do you think James was referring to?

- According to James, how is a demon's faith more sincere than that of some people (v. 19)? What does James say about a "foolish person" who has a mere demon-like faith with no works (v. 20)?

- According to the Scripture, what happened immediately after "Abraham believed God" (v. 23)? Read Eph. 2:8-9. How are these verses consistent with what Abraham experienced after he believed God?

- Abraham was made righteous after he believed, but what evidence did he give later to show that his faith was real (v. 21)? What evidence did the former prostitute Rahab give to show that her faith was real (v. 25)?

- In conclusion, James would agree that believers are saved by faith, but what strong statement does he make about faith "apart from works" (v. 26)?

- Read Matt. 7:19-20. How are James' words consistent with those of Jesus? How does this confront us with *an attitude to change* concerning genuine faith? In your own life, what fruit or works give evidence of genuine saving faith? If there is no evidence of genuine faith, what should a person do?

PRAYER:

Let's pray today that our genuine faith will produce more and more spiritual fruit and works that glorify our Lord.

PRAYER REQUESTS:

BI-MONTHLY MISSION PROJECT NOTES:

WEEK 45

Weekly Bible Reading: .... James 4 – 1 Peter 3
Weekly Bible Study: .... 1 Peter 2:1-10

JAMES 4   [CIRCLE ONE: S P A C E]
Personal Study Notes: _____

_____

_____

_____

JAMES 5   [CIRCLE ONE: S P A C E]
Personal Study Notes: _____

_____

_____

_____

1 PETER 1   [CIRCLE ONE: S P A C E]
Personal Study Notes: _____

_____

_____

_____

1 PETER 2   [CIRCLE ONE: S P A C E]
Personal Study Notes: _____

_____

_____

_____

1 PETER 3   [CIRCLE ONE: S P A C E]
Personal Study Notes: _____

_____

_____

_____

Read carefully one chapter of the Bible five days a week. In each chapter look for a . . .
Sin to Confess / **P**romise to Claim / **A**ttitude to Change / **C**ommand to Obey / **E**xample to Follow.

LONGING FOR GOD'S WORD
(1 PETER 2:1-10)

WEEKLY ASSIGNMENTS:

Lead Prayer Time: _____

Tell the Story (Paraphrase): _____

Read the Text: _____

Facilitate Bible Study: _____

DISCUSSION QUESTIONS:

- How strong is a newborn baby's desire for his or her mother's milk? Why would you be concerned if a baby did not crave the mother's milk?

- In our text, Peter instructed believers on spiritual growth and service. What five things did Peter say we should "put away" as believers (v. 1)? How would you define these five words?

- What did Peter say we should "long for" as believers (v. 2)? What is "pure spiritual milk" and how do we get it? How does spiritual milk help us "grow up into salvation?" How intense is your current desire for God's Word?

- In what ways have you tasted that the Lord is good and gracious (v. 3)? What impact does the Lord's goodness have on your life today?

- Why do you think Peter called Jesus "a Living Stone" (v. 4)? Who are the ones who rejected this "Living Stone?" Who are the ones that are coming to Him?

- When we come to Jesus, in what ways do believers become like "living stones" (v. 5)? What kind of "spiritual house" are we being built up to become? According to Peter, what is the purpose of this "spiritual house?"

- In a building project, what is the significance of a "cornerstone?" Why did Peter call Jesus a chosen and precious "cornerstone" (v. 6)? What did Peter say would never happen to those who believe in Him? In what ways and to whom is Jesus Christ a "stone of stumbling and a rock of offense" (v. 7-8)?

- As believers in Christ, what does it mean that we are a "chosen race" and a "royal priesthood" (v. 9a)? What does it mean that we are a "holy nation" and a "people for His own possession" (v. 9b)? As *a command to obey*, in what ways do you proclaim the excellencies of Christ (v. 9c)?

- Can you share a testimony of how God has "called you out of darkness into His marvelous light" (v. 9d)? Are there any areas of darkness you continue struggle with and how can we pray for you about this?

PRAYER:

Let's pray for one another today as we continue to grow as God's special people.

PRAYER REQUESTS:

BI-MONTHLY MISSION PROJECT NOTES:

WEEK

Weekly Bible Reading: ....1 Peter 4 – 2 Peter 3
Weekly Bible Study: ....2 Peter 3:1-13

1 PETER 4   [CIRCLE ONE: S P A C E]

Personal Study Notes: _____

_____

_____

_____

1 PETER 5   [CIRCLE ONE: S P A C E]

Personal Study Notes: _____

_____

_____

_____

2 PETER 1   [CIRCLE ONE: S P A C E]

Personal Study Notes: _____

_____

_____

_____

2 PETER 2   [CIRCLE ONE: S P A C E]

Personal Study Notes: _____

_____

_____

_____

2 PETER 3   [CIRCLE ONE: S P A C E]

Personal Study Notes: _____

_____

_____

_____

Read carefully one chapter of the Bible five days a week. In each chapter look for a . . .
Sin to Confess / **P**romise to Claim / **A**ttitude to Change / **C**ommand to Obey / **E**xample to Follow.

THE COMING DAY OF THE LORD
(2 PETER 3:1-13)

WEEKLY ASSIGNMENTS:

Lead Prayer Time: _____

Tell the Story (Paraphrase): _____

Read the Text: _____

Facilitate Bible Study: _____

DISCUSSION QUESTIONS:

- Is it possible to know when Jesus will return? Why do you think people try to predict the date that He will return? What can we know about His return?

- In our text, Peter taught believers about the coming day of the Lord. What did Peter say about "scoffers" in the last days (v. 3)? What will these scoffers say and what fact did Peter say they "deliberately overlook" (v. 4-6)? What certain fate did Peter say awaits the present heavens and earth (v. 7)?

- How did Peter describe the difference between time in eternity and time on earth (v. 8)? How does this help you understand God's timing related to your own life?

- According to Peter, why has God delayed in His coming judgment on earth (v. 9)? What does this indicate about the love and grace of God?

- Why do you think Peter compared the coming "day of the Lord" to the coming of a thief (v. 10)? In spite of God's warnings of the coming day of judgment, why do you think many are still not prepared for it? What can we do to help people prepare for this coming day?

- How did Peter describe the "day of the Lord" once it finally arrives (v. 10)? Will anything on earth remain after the coming of this day?

- How close do you think we are to the coming of this day? Knowing this day is coming, according to Peter, what sort of people should we be (v. 11-12)?

- As God's children, what *promise can we claim* and look forward to after the Day of Judgment (v. 13)? What did Peter say would be different about the new heavens and new earth?

- Are you ready for the coming day of the Lord? Why or why not? Are you living right now like it could be today? Who is one person you need to warn about this coming day and pray for his or her salvation?

PRAYER:

Let's pray today that we will witness and live as though the day of the Lord could come today.

PRAYER REQUESTS:

BI-MONTHLY MISSION PROJECT NOTES:

Weekly Bible Reading: . . . . .1 John 1-5
Weekly Bible Study: . . . . .1 John 3:1-10

1 JOHN 1   [CIRCLE ONE: S P A C E]
Personal Study Notes: _____
_____
_____
_____

1 JOHN 2   [CIRCLE ONE: S P A C E]
Personal Study Notes: _____
_____
_____
_____

1 JOHN 3   [CIRCLE ONE: S P A C E]
Personal Study Notes: _____
_____
_____
_____

1 JOHN 4   [CIRCLE ONE: S P A C E]
Personal Study Notes: _____
_____
_____
_____

1 JOHN 5   [CIRCLE ONE: S P A C E]
Personal Study Notes: _____
_____
_____
_____

Read carefully one chapter of the Bible five days a week. In each chapter look for a . . .
Sin to Confess / **P**romise to Claim / **A**ttitude to Change / **C**ommand to Obey / **E**xample to Follow.

CHILDREN OF GOD
(1 JOHN 3:1-10)

WEEKLY ASSIGNMENTS:

Lead Prayer Time: _____

Tell the Story (Paraphrase): _____

Read the Text: _____

Facilitate Bible Study: _____

DISCUSSION QUESTIONS:

- As a child, what was your relationship like with your father? Why is it important for children to have a loving father?

- In our text, John talks about the wonderful privilege of being a child of God. What does it mean to you to be a "child of God?" As a child of God, what kind of love does the Heavenly Father have for you? Read John 1:11-13. What must we do to become children of God?

- According to John, we are "God's children now" (v. 2), but why do we still make mistakes? What does John say will happen to us when Christ appears at His second coming? How awesome will it be to see Christ as He is? Because of this great *promise to claim*, what should we do now (v. 3)?

- What did John say that sin is (v. 4)? What do you think John means by saying, "No one who abides in Him keeps on sinning" (v. 6)? What is the difference between habitually practicing sin and making sinful mistakes? What did John say about the person who "makes a practice of sinning" (v. 8a)?

- According to John, how long has the devil been sinning (v. 8b)? What did John say was the reason the Son of God appeared (v. 8c)? How and in what ways did Jesus come to "destroy the works of the devil (v. 8d)?

- What two reasons did John give for saying, "No one born of God makes a practice of sinning" (v. 9)? As God's children, what is "God's Seed" that abides in us and why can we not "keep on sinning?" Does this mean that we will be perfect and never make sinful mistakes? Why or why not?

- According to John, what two kinds of children are in the world and what two ways can you to tell them apart (v. 10)? Based on the evidence of your life, which kind of child are you? What evidence is there to support your answer? How can children of the devil become children of God (see John 1:11-13)?

PRAYER:

Let's pray today that each of us will continue to sin less and love more.

PRAYER REQUESTS:

BI-MONTHLY MISSION PROJECT NOTES:

WEEK

Weekly Bible Reading: . . . . .2 John 1 – Revelation 2
Weekly Bible Study: . . . . Revelation 2:1-7

2 JOHN 1   [CIRCLE ONE: S P A C E]
Personal Study Notes: _____
_____
_____
_____

3 JOHN 1   [CIRCLE ONE: S P A C E]
Personal Study Notes: _____
_____
_____
_____

JUDE 1   [CIRCLE ONE: S P A C E]
Personal Study Notes: _____
_____
_____
_____

REVELATION 1   [CIRCLE ONE: S P A C E]
Personal Study Notes: _____
_____
_____
_____

REVELATION 2   [CIRCLE ONE: S P A C E]
Personal Study Notes: _____
_____
_____
_____

Read carefully one chapter of the Bible five days a week. In each chapter look for a . . .
Sin to Confess / **P**romise to Claim / **A**ttitude to Change / **C**ommand to Obey / **E**xample to Follow.

LOSING YOUR FIRST LOVE
(REVELATION 2:1-7)

WEEKLY ASSIGNMENTS:

Lead Prayer Time: _____

Tell the Story (Paraphrase): _____

Read the Text: _____

Facilitate Bible Study: _____

DISCUSSION QUESTIONS:

- Why do you enjoy receiving a letter from someone you love? How would you read this letter differently from a business letter?

- In our text, Jesus writes the first of seven letters to seven different churches. Why do you think Jesus wrote these letters to "seven" specific congregations? How awesome would it be to receive a letter from Jesus? What significance do these letters have for us today?

- What good things did Jesus know about the church at Ephesus (v. 1-3)? Why is it good to "not bear with those who are evil?" Do you think the church today is too tolerant of evil? Why or why not? How can a church maintain the balance of showing Christ-like love without being tolerant of sin?

- What one thing did Jesus have against the church at Ephesus (v. 4)? What does it mean to "lose your first love" for Christ? How can a person lose one's first love for Christ, but continue to go through the motions of religious duty?

- How can you tell when you have "first love" for Christ? What spiritual disciplines can you practice to help you maintain your first love for Christ? What three-fold remedy did Jesus give to the church at Ephesus to heal their love problem (v. 5a)? Reflecting on this, is there a *sin to confess*?

- What did Jesus say would happen to the church at Ephesus if they did not repent and return to their first love for Him (v. 5b)? What do you think it means for Christ to remove your lampstand?

- What did Jesus say that we should do with our ears (v. 7)? How do we learn to listen to "the Spirit?" As you consider Jesus' words in this letter, what is the Spirit saying to you today?

PRAYER:

Let's pray for one another today, that our love and passion for Jesus will grow more fervent every day.

PRAYER REQUESTS:

BI-MONTHLY MISSION PROJECT NOTES:

WEEK

Weekly Bible Reading: .... Revelation 3-7
Weekly Bible Study: .... Revelation 3:14-22

REVELATION 3   [CIRCLE ONE: S P A C E]
Personal Study Notes: _____
_____
_____
_____

REVELATION 4   [CIRCLE ONE: S P A C E]
Personal Study Notes: _____
_____
_____
_____

REVELATION 5   [CIRCLE ONE: S P A C E]
Personal Study Notes: _____
_____
_____
_____

REVELATION 6   [CIRCLE ONE: S P A C E]
Personal Study Notes: _____
_____
_____
_____

REVELATION 7   [CIRCLE ONE: S P A C E]
Personal Study Notes: _____
_____
_____
_____

Read carefully one chapter of the Bible five days a week. In each chapter look for a . . .
Sin to Confess / **P**romise to Claim / **A**ttitude to Change / **C**ommand to Obey / **E**xample to Follow.

LUKEWARM COMMITMENT
(REVELATION 3:14-22)

WEEKLY ASSIGNMENTS:

Lead Prayer Time: _____

Tell the Story (Paraphrase): _____

Read the Text: _____

Facilitate Bible Study: _____

DISCUSSION QUESTIONS:

- We like hot drinks and cold drinks, but why do we not like lukewarm drinks? What do you usually do when you drink something lukewarm?

- In our text, Jesus wrote a personal and challenging letter to the church in Laodicea. What did Jesus know about the spiritual commitment of the people in this church (v. 15)? Why do you think He would rather for them to either be cold or hot in their commitment to Him?

- How would you describe lukewarm commitment to Christ? What did Jesus say He would do because of their lukewarm commitment (v. 16)? What do you think He meant by this?

- What did the people of this church say about themselves (v. 17)? How is their view of themselves different from that of Christ? Do you think most churches today see themselves different from how Christ sees them? Why or why not?

- What was Jesus' counsel to the church in Laodicea (v. 18)? What two things did Jesus promise to those whom He loves (v. 19)? Why are these two things unpleasant but necessary? In what ways have you experienced these two things in your personal relationship with Christ?

- What did Jesus mean by saying, "I stand at the door and knock" (v. 20)? What did He say He would do for those who hear and open the door? As a *promise to claim*, what did Jesus say He would do for those who conquer (v. 21)?

- Today, would you say your commitment to Christ is cold, hot, or lukewarm? How can we maintain a burning hot commitment to Christ? What would you say is the spiritual temperature of your church? What can you do to fan the flames of your church's commitment to Christ?

PRAYER:

Let's pray for one another today, that our love and passion for Jesus will grow more fervent every day.

PRAYER REQUESTS:

BI-MONTHLY MISSION PROJECT NOTES:

WEEK

Weekly Bible Reading: .... Revelation 8-12
Weekly Bible Study: .... Revelation 10:1-11

REVELATION 8   [CIRCLE ONE: S P A C E]
Personal Study Notes: _____
_____
_____
_____

REVELATION 9   [CIRCLE ONE: S P A C E]
Personal Study Notes: _____
_____
_____
_____

REVELATION 10   [CIRCLE ONE: S P A C E]
Personal Study Notes: _____
_____
_____
_____

REVELATION 11   [CIRCLE ONE: S P A C E]
Personal Study Notes: _____
_____
_____
_____

REVELATION 12   [CIRCLE ONE: S P A C E]
Personal Study Notes: _____
_____
_____
_____

Read carefully one chapter of the Bible five days a week. In each chapter look for a . . .
Sin to Confess / **P**romise to Claim / **A**ttitude to Change / **C**ommand to Obey / **E**xample to Follow.

THE BITTERSWEET SCROLL
(REVELATION 10:1-11)

WEEKLY ASSIGNMENTS:

Lead Prayer Time: _____

Tell the Story (Paraphrase): _____

Read the Text: _____

Facilitate Bible Study: _____

DISCUSSION QUESTIONS:

- When is the last time you saw a beautiful rainbow? What do you think about when you see a rainbow?

- In our text, a mighty angel with a rainbow over his head announced that there would be no more delay concerning the return of Jesus Christ. What is the significance of the rainbow in relation to the return of Christ? Read Genesis 9:11-17. How is the rainbow related to God's promise to Noah?

- What did the mighty angel do with His right foot and His left foot (v. 2-4)? What do you think is the significance of his actions? What do you think is the significance of the seven thunders? What was John instructed to do concerning the seven thunders, and why do you think he was told to do this?

- When the mighty angel raised his right hand to heaven and swore by Him who lives forever and forever, what specific announcement did he make (v. 5-7)? Why do you think the return of Christ has been delayed until this announcement? Read 2 Peter 3:9-10. What did Peter say about this?

- What was John instructed to do with the scroll that was open in the hand of the mighty angel (v. 8-10)? What was John told the scroll would do in his stomach? What was John told the scroll would taste like in his mouth?

- What do you think is the significance of this bittersweet scroll? What will be bitter about the end times and the return of Christ? What will be sweet about the return of Christ?

- If Jesus were to return today, who do you know that would be left behind to face the bitterness of God's judgment? If Jesus returned today, who do you know in heaven with whom you would have a sweet and eternal reunion?

- Why do you think John was told, "You must prophesy again about many peoples and nations and languages and kings" (v. 11)? Why is it important for us to tell others about Jesus and His return? Who do you need to tell soon?

PRAYER:

Let's pray today for one another that our witness for Christ will be more fervent and passionate than ever before?

PRAYER REQUESTS:

BI-MONTHLY MISSION PROJECT NOTES:

Weekly Bible Reading: .... Revelation 13-17
Weekly Bible Study: .... Revelation 13:11-18

REVELATION 13   [CIRCLE ONE: S P A C E]
Personal Study Notes: _____
_____
_____
_____

REVELATION 14   [CIRCLE ONE: S P A C E]
Personal Study Notes: _____
_____
_____
_____

REVELATION 15   [CIRCLE ONE: S P A C E]
Personal Study Notes: _____
_____
_____
_____

REVELATION 16   [CIRCLE ONE: S P A C E]
Personal Study Notes: _____
_____
_____
_____

REVELATION 17   [CIRCLE ONE: S P A C E]
Personal Study Notes: _____
_____
_____
_____

Read carefully one chapter of the Bible five days a week. In each chapter look for a . . .
Sin to Confess / **P**romise to Claim / **A**ttitude to Change / **C**ommand to Obey / **E**xample to Follow.

THE ANTICHRIST AND HIS PROPHET
(REVELATION 13:11-18)

WEEKLY ASSIGNMENTS:

Lead Prayer Time: _____

Tell the Story (Paraphrase): _____

Read the Text: _____

Facilitate Bible Study: _____

DISCUSSION QUESTIONS:

• What do you think of when you hear the word Antichrist? What do you think of when you see the number 666?

• In our text, John tells about two individuals described as beasts that will rise up before Christ's return. The first beast is the Antichrist and the second is his false prophet. Why is it important for us to know about these two beasts?

• As John described the second beast, which is the false prophet, what did he look like (v. 11)? Who did he speak like? Read Revelation 12: 9. Who is this "dragon" that he spoke like? Why do you think he looked like a lamb? How does this present an *attitude to change* about trusting every prophet?

• What does John say the false prophet will make the inhabitants of earth do with the first beast, which is the

Antichrist (v. 12)? How is he able to do this (v. 13-14)? By what miraculous deception does the false prophet turn the Antichrist into a counterfeit image of Jesus Christ (v. 15)?

- What will happen to those who refuse to worship the image of the Antichrist (v. 15b)? What will all people, including the small and great, rich and poor, free and slave, be required to do (v. 16)? What will all people on earth be unable to do without the mark of the beast (v. 17)?

- With today's technology, how easy would it be to administer the mark of the beast? How do you think this mark would be administered and what arguments could be raised to justify its necessity? Do you think people today would easily fall for these arguments? Why or why not?

- What does the number 666 represent (v. 18)? Why do you think this number is the "number of the beast?"

- Why must we be cautious not to become carried away with silly predictions concerning the Antichrist and his mark? On the other hand, why do you think God revealed this truth to us and what can we take away from it? To identify deception when you see it, why is it vital for you to study and to know truth?

PRAYER:

Let's pray today for a greater hunger for God's truth and for greater discernment when dealing with deception.

PRAYER REQUESTS:

BI-MONTHLY MISSION PROJECT NOTES:

WEEK 52

Weekly Bible Reading: .... Revelation 18-22
Weekly Bible Study: .... Revelation 21:1-8, 22-27

REVELATION 18   [CIRCLE ONE: S P A C E]

Personal Study Notes: _____

_____

_____

_____

REVELATION 19   [CIRCLE ONE: S P A C E]

Personal Study Notes: _____

_____

_____

_____

REVELATION 20   [CIRCLE ONE: S P A C E]

Personal Study Notes: _____

_____

_____

_____

REVELATION 21   [CIRCLE ONE: S P A C E]

Personal Study Notes: _____

_____

_____

_____

REVELATION 22   [CIRCLE ONE: S P A C E]

Personal Study Notes: _____

_____

_____

_____

Read carefully one chapter of the Bible five days a week. In each chapter look for a . . .
Sin to Confess / **P**romise to Claim / **A**ttitude to Change / **C**ommand to Obey / **E**xample to Follow.

ETERNAL LIFE IN HEAVEN
(REVELATION 21:1-8, 22-27)

WEEKLY ASSIGNMENTS:

Lead Prayer Time: _____

Tell the Story (Paraphrase): _____

Read the Text: _____

Facilitate Bible Study: _____

DISCUSSION QUESTIONS:

- How would life be different if there was no promise of eternal life in heaven? Why do you think God chose to tell us about heaven?

- In our text, John described the beauty of heaven. Why is it significant that there will be "no more sea" in the new heaven and earth (v. 1)? Since there will be no more sea to divide us, how does it make you feel that in heaven you will never be separated from your loved ones again?

- What is implied by the description of the new Jerusalem as being like "a bride adorned for her husband" (v. 2)? What is more beautiful than a bride? What do you think it will be like to live in the very presence of God (v. 3)?

- What specific things did John say will "be no more" when we get to heaven (v. 4)? How does this encourage you in facing trials? Read Romans 8:18. What can we know about the sufferings of this present time?

- What great *promises to claim* are spoken by Him "who was seated on the throne (v. 5-7)? According to John, what people will not be in heaven (v. 8a)? Where will these people spend eternity in the "second death" (v. 8b)?

- Why will there be no temple in heaven (v. 22)? Why is there no sun or moon (v. 23)? Why do you think the gates of heaven are never shut (v. 24-25)? What will the people of heaven bring into the gates of heaven (v. 26)?

- In verse 8, we saw those who will not be in heaven, but who are the only ones who will enter the gates of heaven (v. 27)? Who is the Lamb and what did He do for us so that we could be in His book?

- How can you know that your name is written in the Lamb's book of life? If you know this, how should this change the way you live on earth?

PRAYER:

Let's pray for one another to live everyday on earth for the One who died so that we could have eternal life heaven.

PRAYER REQUESTS:

BI-MONTHLY MISSION PROJECT NOTES:

AUTHOR BIO

Dr. Bill Wilks has served as pastor of Northpark Baptist Church in Trussville, Alabama, for over fifteen years. He is passionate about making and multiplying disciples, and has trained thousands of believers across the globe in disciple-making using D-Life. Email Dr. Wilks for leadership training for D-Life at bill.wilks@me.com. For additional help and encouragement for using and living D-Life, check out:

- The D-Life Website at www.livingthedlife.com
- The D-Life Blog at www.livingthedlife.com/category/d-life-blog/
- Living the D-Life Facebook Page at www.facebook.com/livingthedlife
- Twitter at www.twitter.com/BillWilks